PAR

NF

Advance Praise for *Borough Market: Edible Histories*

'The story of Borough Market mirrors the British food revolution. This book tells that story; deliciously, ingredient by ingredient.' – William Sitwell

'This is the perfect book for those moments when you find yourself in the kitchen wondering about how a particular ingredient found its way into our everyday culinary lives. It's as enticing as Borough Market always is, as witty as Mark Riddaway always is, and packed with the kind of knowledge I love.' – Angela Clutton

'Fascinating and entertaining – a pleasure to read.' – Claudia Roden

'It's so important that Borough and the food community are supported, and what better way of spreading the word than through the stories and histories of a most historic market that has become a unique beacon of good things.' – Jeremy Lee

'This book is for lovers of food and markets and history. It's also a book that everyone who eats should read. It is fascinating, informative and entertaining. Mark Riddaway effortlessly guides us through Borough, telling the story of the market and its produce with ease and grace.' – Kay Plunkett-Hogge

'Mark Riddaway's *Edible Histories* is thoroughly researched and engagingly written and belongs on the shelf of anyone interested in food history. Even if you are not interested, this is the book that will get you started.' – Mark Kurlansky

ABOUT THE AUTHOR

Mark Riddaway is an award-winning writer, editor and publisher. Through his independent publishing company, LSC Publishing, he has launched, edited and written for a host of highly regarded magazines and websites, covering subjects as diverse as food, culture, weather, parenting and the Marylebone district of London. His involvement with Borough Market began more than a decade ago, and since 2012 he has been the editor and publisher of *Market Life*, the Market's bi-monthly food magazine, which among numerous accolades was named Best Food Magazine or Section by the Guild of Food Writers in both 2018 and 2019. In 2020, Mark's regular columns in *Market Life* earned him a place on the Guild's shortlist for its food writing award.

BOROUGH MARKET
EDIBLE HISTORIES

Epic Tales *of*
Everyday Ingredients

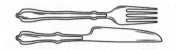

MARK RIDDAWAY

HODDER &
STOUGHTON

First published in Great Britain in 2020 by Hodder & Stoughton
An Hachette UK company

1

Copyright © The Trustees of The Borough Market (Southwark) 2020

The right of Mark Riddaway to be identified as the Author of the
Work has been asserted by him in accordance with the Copyright,
Designs and Patents Act 1988.

A CIP catalogue record for this title is available from the British Library

Illustrations by Emily Langford

Hardback ISBN 978 1 529 34970 2
eBook ISBN 978 1 529 34971 9

Typeset in Sabon LT Std by
Palimpsest Book Production Ltd, Falkirk, Stirlingshire

Printed and bound in Great Britain by Clays Ltd, Elcograf S.p.A.

Hodder & Stoughton policy is to use papers that are natural,
renewable and recyclable products and made from wood
grown in sustainable forests. The logging and manufacturing
processes are expected to conform to the environmental
regulations of the country of origin.

Hodder & Stoughton Ltd
Carmelite House
50 Victoria Embankment
London EC4Y 0DZ

www.hodder.co.uk

CONTENTS

INTRODUCTION

'Know where your food
comes from.'

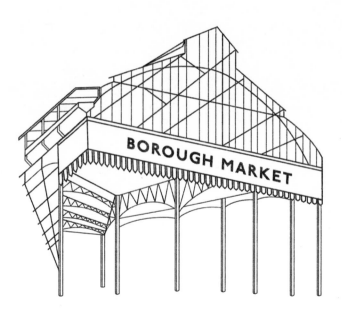

'KNOW WHERE YOUR FOOD COMES from.' For almost a decade now, I've had the great pleasure of writing for and editing Borough Market's magazine, *Market Life*. Throughout that time, the call to better understand the provenance of our food has been put out again and again by just about every food producer, merchant, chef, campaigner and food policy expert whose thoughts have been shared through the publication's pages. In fact, challenge me to distil the essence of Borough Market into six words or fewer, and this entreaty is probably the closest I'd get to a satisfactory solution. Either that or: 'Try the x [x being the most recent purchase to have made angels dance upon my tongue], it is amazing,' (although this would usually bust my six-word limit by demanding a colourful adjective, Anglo-Saxon in origin, inserted before 'amazing').

Borough, London's most famous food market, is a wonderfully chaotic place populated by a kaleidoscopic cast of traders, but it's a collective bound by a common thread: the ability to shine a light into – and build bridges across – the deep canyon that too often separates us from the source of our food. In recent decades, the increasingly monolithic, impersonal nature of the British food industry has cut us off from the world of farmers, bakers, fishermen and cheesemakers – and despite the convenience it brings, that's really not a good thing. If you don't know who made your food, if you don't understand the method of its production or the long, mazy route it travelled to get to you, it is hard to know what harm it may have caused and whether you're being completely short-changed by its taste. Because of this disconnect, it's all too easy to presume you're eating something pure and wholesome when really it's fifty per cent ultra-processed rubbish and fifty per cent marketing. You can be gulled into thinking that all salmon is a bit slimy, that cheddar cheese is a dull, plasticised mass, and that carrots don't taste of very much. And in extreme circumstances, as recent history has shown, you can be led to believe you're eating British beef when you're actually eating Romanian horse.

Borough's approach – like that of many farmers' markets and independent shops – is to shorten those byzantine supply chains and bring conversations about quality, sustainability, waste, environmental degradation and fair pay out into the light. Shop here and there's a high chance that the person serving you produced the food with their own hands, or is employed directly by the people who did. Traders who aren't producers themselves are on close speaking terms (and probably eating and drinking terms) with the people who supply them: a connection forged through a shared obsession with the food in question. Visit their stalls and they'll tell you, with infectious enthusiasm, everything you need to know. They'll give you the confidence that what you're buying satisfies both your conscience and your palate.

If you want to eat well, there's no such thing as too much knowledge, just as (to my mind at least) there's no such thing as too much cheese. While markets like Borough clearly can't provide all the answers to the problems within our food system, they can at least help us figure out what the right questions are.

This book takes that healthy hunger for knowledge and runs with it, back through the centuries. It started with the idea that a modicum of enlightenment – and a great deal of entertainment – could be found in learning not just how a particular ingredient found its way to a market stall or supermarket shelf, but how its forebears passed through space and time to exist in this form, in this place, in this moment: knowing not just where our food comes from, but where our food really *comes from*.

The seeds of its creation were planted a few years ago with a suggestion by the Borough Market team that we commission a food historian to write a regular column about the past life of some of the ingredients available at the Market. But why, I asked, with persuasive logic, would we fork out for an established professional historian when we have, right here in the room, a man obsessed with both food and history who would attack such an undertaking with breathless enthusiasm? And so, excited by the thought that my master's degree in medieval history (attained decades earlier as a way of delaying for a year the inevitable upgrade of my part-time office temp job to a full-time one) might prove against all the odds to have been a useful vocational qualification, I started researching the history of the potato. Ever since then, I've been buried up to my neck in classical medicine, medieval farming, Elizabethan herbalism and Victorian horticulture.

Through my *Market Life* column, I've explored the biographies of almost forty different ingredients, and the journey of discovery has been a source of near-constant delight – something I hope comes across in my writing. It's the richness of it all that blows my mind: food is fundamental to the mundane passage of our daily lives, but it also drives many of the grand narratives of human progress. The history of food is the history of everything, big or small. It's the history of science, medicine and philosophy. It's the history of war, migration, cultural exchange, trade, colonisation, enslavement and environmental destruction. It's the history of celebration and self-indulgence, of hunger and grim sustenance. It's the history of disgusted expressions and aching stomachs. All human life is here, licking its plate clean, laughing and farting.

These stories now make up about ninety per cent of my dinner table conversation. Put any food or drink in front of me and there's a high chance it'll trigger some rambling disquisition about the key role played in the evolution of the strawberry by a French spy whose surname was Strawberry; why hunters tended to shoot wild turkeys from the lower branches of a tree first; or the deep unease felt by sixteenth-century Persian rhubarb merchants at the prospect of Europeans drinking tea. If all goes to plan, you'll soon be rambling on about these things too.

Edible Histories is a collection of some of my favourite stories, not necessarily history's most important foods (potatoes, bread, salt, cod and citrus fruits would demand inclusion if that were the case), nor those that I most enjoy eating (although definitely some of those), but a somewhat free-wheeling selection that offers a good spread of ingredients and a balance between depressing narratives and lighter fare. Much to my relief, the book has given me the space to get deeper into these tales than the magazine's tight word limit ever allowed (honestly, trying to condense six thousand years of the onion into a few hundred words was as hard as condensing six thousand onions into an average-sized cooking pot, and drew tears just as readily). Still, these essays barely touch the surface.

My intention has been to produce something fast and fun, seasoned with the merest soupçon of profundity. If anything stays with you beyond a few interesting facts to share at the dinner table, I hope it's the sense that what we choose to eat and drink does matter. Europe's appetite for coffee played a significant role in the disgusting institution of slavery, the human costs of which continue to accumulate. Completely unconsciously, every Briton who fell in love with tea in the seventeenth century helped in some small way to precipitate a revolution in America, a war with China and the ruthless exploitation of India. The Catholic Church's penchant for dried fish financed the rise of the Dutch empire, while Venice was built on the medieval belief that spices not only made food taste good but enhanced the strength of men's erections. No matter how trivial an individual's shopping and dining habits may have seemed in the moment, their aggregation had the power to shape history. Our appetites dictated what was grown, reared or pulled from the seas and what was propelled around the planet – and that in turn had a profound impact on the world.

Today, we hold the same power to shape the future as those Restoration tea-drinkers unknowingly wielded. If we let our old apple varieties disappear because of the supermarkets' insistence upon humdrum sameness, they'll be gone forever. If we continue to eat too much cheap, intensively reared meat, there's a good chance that when history is being written from the arid Mad Max-style wastelands of the future, that choice will appear somewhat less reasonable than it does now. If we pull fish from our seas in a manner that isn't sustainable, our descendants, denied the pleasures of a vinegary bag of fish and chips, won't judge us kindly. In short, it's good to know where our food comes from because, if we do, we'll have a much better chance of knowing where it's headed.

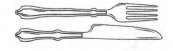

APPLES

W E BEGIN, AS AT LEAST one other major book does, in the Garden of Eden.

Picture it now: Eve, naked and pensive beside a tree, forbidden fruit in hand; a snake, its tongue flickering, goading her to take a bite. If your homeland happens to be Britain – or plenty of other places besides – the fruit you see won't be a banana. It's not a strawberry, a pear or a plum. It's an apple.

This familiar tableau tells us more about the apple than it does about Eden. In the original text of the Bible, the forbidden fruit was just that: a fruit (*peri* in Hebrew). Jewish scholars generally pointed towards contenders better suited to a Levantine setting – a citron, a grape or a fig – and in the greatest of all biblical paintings, Michelangelo's Sistine Chapel fresco in Rome, it's a fig tree around which the serpent is coiled. And yet, from the medieval period on, barely a single depiction of Eden created north of the Alps, from *The Last Judgment* by Hieronymus Bosch (c.1482) to John Milton's *Paradise Lost* (1667) to the stained glass windows of just about every church, has featured a fruit other than an apple.

And it's not just in Eve's hand that the apple has endured

as a symbol of sin, sex, knowledge and beauty. Think of the golden apples stolen by the Greek god Atlas; the Apple of Discord, which sparked the Trojan wars; the youth-giving apples of the Norse goddess Idun; the poisoned fruits of Thomas Malory's *Le Morte d'Arthur* (1485) and the Grimm brothers' *Snow White* (1812); those shot from various innocent heads by the Danish Palnatoki, the Northumbrian Adam Bell and the Swiss William Tell. Even accounting for the fact that in many European languages the word for an apple was once applied more generically to any fleshy seed-bearing fruit, it is fair to say that neither the peach nor the quince ever came loaded with quite the same allegorical punch.

That we see apples in our imagined paradise is partly a product of that resounding cultural echo, partly a reflection of their polished beauty but mainly because, as the centuries passed, we became increasingly used to seeing them everywhere: in our orchards, in our woods and hedgerows, in our markets. We placed an apple into Eve's hand because in northern Europe, where an apple can be bought on any day on every high street, what else could possibly spring to mind?

The real story of the apple began not in the Garden of Eden but on the slopes of the Tian Shan, a mountain range that rolls across central Asia. Although shrinking in the face of relentless development, it remains a place of stunning biodiversity, including in some forested areas a multitude of extraordinary wild apple trees. It was in the Kazakh sector of the range, in 1929, that Nikolai Ivanovich Vavilov, the brilliant Soviet plant geneticist (far too brilliant for Stalin, who had him thrown in prison, where he died in 1943), claimed to have uncovered the birthplace of *Malus domestica*, the domesticated apple. Vavilov wrote: 'It is possible to see with our own eyes that we are in the centre of origin of the cultivated apple, where wild apples were difficult to even distinguish from those which were being cultivated. Some of the wild ecotypes in these forests were so superior in quality and size that they could be taken directly from an orchard to market without anyone knowing the difference.' He was right. Those wild apples, a species known as *Malus sieversii*, have been shown through DNA analysis to be the principal ancestors of all the domesticated apples that spill from super-market shelves and works of religious art.

As these beautiful fruits were dispersed and domesticated beyond the Tian Shan, they met with other wild apples whose DNA inveigled itself into the gene pool. Conspicuous among these was the crab apple (*Malus sylvestris*) – plentiful and widely dispersed but forbiddingly hard and astringently tart (as the Roman naturalist Pliny the Elder wrote, its sourness 'will even take the edge off a knife'). Recent exca-vations at a gravel quarry in Worcestershire uncovered a fire pit containing stone axe-heads, flint tools, barley grains and a large quantity of charred crab apples dating from around 2900–2600 BCE, all of which were chucked into the flames with some ritual purpose in mind – an early indication that the cultural significance of these brutally acidic fruits far surpassed their usefulness as a food. Their significance would live on in Britain's pagan myths and rites, vestiges of which linger today in Yuletide wassailing and Halloween apple bobbing.

In stark contrast, the scions of *Malus sieversii* were so big and sweet that growing and eating them would prove far preferable to lobbing them into fire pits, hence their gradual dissemination. The Tian Shan mountains are close to some of the most important trade and migration routes through the wide lowlands that join Europe with Asia, later known as the Silk Road, and it was along these arteries that apples made their way into the great kingdoms of the Near East. They appeared in the law codes of the Hittites of Anatolia (c.1650–1500 BCE), which determined the financial penalty for anyone whose brush fire accidentally set light to an apple orchard (six shekels per tree, with a discount if the culprit was a slave), and on a tablet from the Assyrian city of Nuzi, dating from around the same time, which made reference to a man called Tupkitilla selling his orchard in exchange for three sheep.

The ancient Persians were experts in horticulture, and the apple enjoyed a prominent place in their gardens. In the Persepolis fortification archive, a set of clay tablets filled with administrative records from the reign of Darius I (509–493 BCE), apple pips were listed conspicuously among the thousands of fruit seeds sent out to five royal estates. Centuries later, Strabo, the Greek geographer and historian, described the apple's role in Persian weddings, alluding to its importance as a symbol as well as a food. 'Marriages are celebrated at the beginning of the vernal equinox,' he wrote. 'The bridegroom passes into the bride-chamber, having previously eaten some apples or camel's marrow but nothing else during the day.' Today, occasions on which camel marrow is suggested as a straight swap for apple are few and far between.

It was through Persia that apples made their way to ancient Greece, where they quickly became part of the cultural language. In *The Odyssey*, Homer imagined 'the most delicious apples' growing in the orchard of King Alcinous, a place where 'the fruits never rot nor fail all the year round, neither winter nor summer'. The Greek essayist Plutarch, in his *Moralia* (c.100 CE), later offered a compelling explanation for Homer's admiration of apples: 'No other fruit unites the fine qualities of all fruits as does the apple. For one thing, its skin is so clean when you touch it that instead of staining the hands it perfumes them. Its taste is sweet and it is extremely delightful both to smell and to look at. Thus, by charming all our senses at once, it deserves the praise that it receives.' Remember that the next time you're biting distractedly into a Gala.

It wasn't just the apples of the Near East that migrated to Greece, but the knowledge needed to cultivate them. Among the many reasons for the species' success is its remarkable genetic variability – a quality known as heterozygosity. Plant all the seeds found within an apple and each tree that results will display different characteristics. This variability means that pips from the most delicious apple in the world have the potential to grow into trees whose fruits are a crushing disappointment. Conversely, an incredible new variety can emerge entirely at random – but, because planting its seeds would trigger another roll of the genetic dice, extending its life beyond that of a single tree requires skilled intervention. Some apple varieties can root from cuttings but, for the most part, the more complex art of grafting – the fusing of the shoots, buds or branches of one tree with the roots or trunk of another – is required for an apple's qualities to live on.

Exactly when and where this ingenious technique first

emerged is lost to us. *On the Nature of the Child*, written around 420 BCE by a follower of the Greek physician Hippocrates, mentioned plants being grafted, as did Theophrastus, a protégé of Aristotle, in his *Enquiry into Plants* (c.350–287 BCE), but its genesis clearly pre-dated such references. Plutarch would later produce a particularly enjoyable description of some extreme inter-species examples: 'Soclarus . . . showed us trees which had been fancified in all sorts of ways by what is called grafting; we saw olives growing upon mastic trees and pomegranates upon the myrtle; and there were oaks which bore good pears, plane trees which had received grafts of apples, and figs grafts of mulberries, and other mixtures of trees mastered to the point of producing fruit. Then the rest of the company began to tease Soclarus for raising, as they said, classes and specimens more marvellous than the sphinxes and chimaeras of the poets.'

When Pliny wrote *The Natural History* (77–79 CE), the art of selectively grafting apples was so developed that Romans were able to choose from a long list of well-established varieties gathered from around the empire, known either for their origins – the Amerina (from Amelia in Umbria), the Syricum ('Syrian'), the Graecula ('little Greek') – or their defining characteristics – the seedless Spadonium ('impotent'), the swollen Pulmoneum ('lung-shaped'), the fast-fading Pannuceum ('shrivelled') and the schoolboy's favourite, Orthomastium ('pert-breasted'). Wealthy Romans were enthusiastic consumers of fresh fruit, which tended to be presented with great display at the end of a meal, and the apple was one of the stars of the show. So set did it become as a way of rounding off a dinner, the phrase '*ab ovo usque ad mala*' ('from the egg to the apples') was used to mean 'from the beginning to the end'.

One of the benefits of the apple's genetic diversity is that some varieties fruit early, others late; some need to be eaten soon after picking while others benefit from being stored for a while, their flesh mellowing and sweetening in the process. Columella, a contemporary of Pliny, described several types that would thrive if stored in a cold loft, 'in a very dry place, where neither smoke nor noisome smell may come,' packed in 'small chests of beech, or of lime tree also, such as senators or judges' robes are laid up in, but somewhat larger'. His one caveat was that, as is sadly true of the world far beyond apples, 'when different kinds are shut up together, they disagree with one another and are much more speedily corrupted and spoiled'.

It was the Romans who introduced the *Malus domestica* to Britain, France and Spain, and the tools they used – the knives and hooks required for pruning and grafting – have been uncovered at many Roman sites across the northern parts of the empire. When the Romans left, the importance afforded to fruit cultivation in the kingdoms they left behind slowly faded. Across Europe, the art of horticulture was kept alive by monks, for whom its synthesis of learning and labour was considered a virtuous one, and later by the Moorish conquerors of Spain and Sicily, the Islamic world having inherited and enhanced the ancient Near East's deep love and understanding of gardens and orchards. Some wealthy landowners, too, remained wedded to the apple's charms. *Capitulare de Villis*, a management manual for the royal estates of Charlemagne, king of the Franks, demanded the planting of apple trees, including several specific varieties ('Gozmaringa, Geroldinga, Crevedella, Spirauca') and a few broad categories: 'Sweet ones, bitter ones, those that keep well, those that are to be eaten straightaway, and early ones.' For the most part, though, in the Romans' wake, the apple became a fruit of the woodland rather than the orchard, consumed in large quantities but mainly through forage rather than fabrication.

As the monastic orders expanded rapidly in the twelfth century, and their horticultural skills were carried far and wide, European fruit growing experienced a renaissance. It was the French who led the way in identifying, propagating and commercialising the most enticing varieties of apple, including the Rouviau, the Blandurel and the Costard. In 1292, the English royal household of Edward I imported three hundred pounds of Costards from France, each one costing four times as much as the unnamed native apples recorded in the same document. After cuttings were brought across the Channel and grafted into English orchards, the Costard would lend its name to the generic word for a fruitseller, which would endure in markets like Borough until deep into the twentieth century: costermonger.

The French influence on the English taste for apples can be seen in John Lydgate's epic poem 'Henry VI's Triumphal Entry into London' (1432), which described displays of fruit trees 'fulle of fruytes lade, / Of colour hevynly.' Among the rare and exotic fruits on show, alongside 'orenges, almondis, and the pomegernade,' Lydgate included two French apple varieties, 'Pypyns' and 'Blaunderell'. Other apples with French origins – 'Costardes,' 'Pomewater and 'gentyll Ricardouns' – were listed among the 'fruytes which more comune be'. Only one of the varieties mentioned in the poem had emerged from England: the Queening or Quoining, the name of which alluded to its angular ridges being like those of a 'quoin', an old spelling of 'coin'. Another early native of these shores was the Pearmain, so called for its pear-like shape. Exchequer records from 1204 noted that the lord of the manor of Runham in Norfolk was liable for an annual tax of two hundred Pearmains and four hogsheads of cider – a transaction that, to the modern reader, appears definitively East Anglian.

Beyond the spacious confines of the monasteries and manor houses, apples were unsuited to the system of open fields that dominated the medieval landscape. The land from which peasants drew their sustenance consisted of vast, unfenced common fields, narrow strips of which were tended to by individual families. As the cultivation of large, slow-maturing fruit trees was simply not practical within these slim plots, the only apples eaten by the poor were nameless and semi-wild, gathered from trees that grew haphazardly on the forested perimeter of the village. The apple's gradual move from the margins only really began when this communal system of agriculture began to be wiped out by the progress of enclosure: the slow transform- ation of the English agricultural system from one of common lands to one dominated by larger, more capitalistic farms on which the establishment of fruit trees became a viable option.

This was particularly true in the west of England. In the counties of the south-east, the flat landscapes and light soils lent themselves to intensive arable farming and the produc- tion of soft fruits for sale in London's voracious food markets, but in the wet, rugged westerly regions, where cereals flourished less readily, apple trees and livestock offered a complementary combination: trees provided natural barriers and shelter for the animals, cider provided both income and in-house intoxication, and the pomace from cider making – the mulch left behind after pressing – could be used as a nutritious form of animal feed.

It wasn't until the Tudor period that commercial apple orchards began to be established away from the cider centres of Devon, Somerset, Gloucestershire and Herefordshire. Richard Harris, Henry VIII's fruiterer, set up a royal fruit collection at Teynham, east Kent, in 1533, when he 'fetched out of Fraunce a great store of graftes, especially Pippins, before which time there were no Pippins in England'. Harris's collection became 'the chiefe mother of all other orchards,' and Pippin – a word used to describe a late-keeping, fine flavoured apple – established itself as one of the defining terms in the English apple lexicon. The expansion of organised fruit growing was accelerated by the arrival in England of green-fingered Protestant refugees from France and Flanders, many of whom settled in Kent and Surrey.

In his famous encyclopaedia of plants, *The Herball* (1597), the Elizabethan botanist John Gerard made brief mention of these orchards. 'The tame and grafted apple trees are planted and set in gardens and orchards made for that purpose: they delight to growe in good and fertile grounds. Kent doth abound with apples of most sortes.' This he contrasted with the abundant but more chaotic apple trees found in the 'pastures and hedge rowes' of Herefordshire's mixed farms, including one estate with so many apples that not only did the staff drink nothing but cider, which was also used as a currency to pay the tithe to the parson, but the pigs who scavenged on fallen fruits had become surprisingly fussy: 'The hogs are fed with the fallings of them, which are so many, that they make choise of those apples they do eate, who will not taste of any but of the best.'

As the presence of apple trees in England's farms, market gardens and orchards multiplied, so too did the abundance of varieties, the naming of which became a very English artform: a beautiful blend of poetry and profanity. John Parkinson, later made royal botanist to Charles I, listed and rated in his *Paradisi in Sole* (1629) more than fifty distinct types, while also dismissing 'twenty sorts of Sweetings, and none good'. His roll call included the Bastard Queene (like the Queene apple but less tasty), the Leathercoate (a small, sharp, winter fruit), the Cat's Head ('took the name of the likeness'), the Cowsnout (as bad as it sounds), the Old Wife (better than it sounds), and the Woman's Breast (a pleasing echo of Pliny).

The best sorts of apple, wrote Parkinson, are good 'at the last course for the table, in most men's houses of account'. This presentation of apples at the end of a meal, alongside other sweet treats – an echo of the Roman way – was the reason why sweet apples, eaten raw rather than cooked into puddings, became known, somewhat confusingly, as dessert apples. The idea that a good apple might be enjoyed straight from the hand was, though, one that for many centuries had remained strangely dormant. Throughout the medieval period, raw apples were widely considered dangerous. There was some logic in this: excessive consumption of fruit can lead to an upset stomach, which could easily be mistaken for the 'fluxes' associated with deadly fevers. Throw in the associated mythos of sin and temptation, and the fact that most old apple varieties, including the Costard, were intensely sharp, and it's easy to see why munching one fresh from the branch would be best avoided.

Instead, apples tended to be cooked. As John Gerard wrote: 'Rosted apples are alwaies better than the rawe, the harme whereof is both mended by the fire, and may also be corrected by adding unto them seedes or spices.' Spices were beyond the reach of most people, but the roasting or baking of apples was commonplace. In William Langland's *Piers Plowman* (c.1370–90), one of the great medieval poems, a list of simple foods with which the very poor would attempt to 'plese' the looming presence of Hunger included 'baken apples'. In London, 'coddled' apples, cooked until soft and pulpy, were created in bakers' ovens after the bread had been made, and were hawked on the streets with the cry 'hot codlins hot'.

The rich could afford to splash out on cinnamon and nutmeg. A recipe for appulmoy – a sweet apple sauce with almond milk and spices – appeared in *The Forme of Cury* (c.1390), a collection of recipes from the court of Richard II. In the same book, a recipe for 'tartys in applis' made clear that apple pie, now a symbol of America, is really as English as, well, just about every other kind of pie – in it, apples came baked in a pastry 'cofyn' with a delicious combination of spices including saffron and figs, raisins and pears. A similar English recipe from around 1425 included the rather more questionable addition of ground-up 'samon, or codlynge, or hadok'. Usually without the fish, that combination of apple and spice has remained integral to English cookery ever since.

The growing appeal of dessert apples did nothing to dent the popularity of baked apples and apple pies, but it did feed a new interest in apple cultivation, certainly among the elite. In the grounds of stately homes, perfectly coiffured apple trees, grown from dwarf rootstocks, trained into elegant shapes – pyramids, cylinders, bells – and laid out in pleasingly formal displays, provided fruits that could be served on silver platters to wealthy guests and cooed over for the subtlety of their perfume. There was a patriotic edge to this fetishisation of fruit, English apples being, of course, so much better than anyone else's. In the nineteenth century, this would feed into the Arts and Crafts movement, an aesthetic reaction to industrialisation, which promoted a romantic, nostalgic vision of rural life, in whose hands the apple – wholesome, beautiful and ancient – became something of a totem.

But for all the esteem in which English apples were held by people with a penchant for silver fruit platters and William Morris textiles, out in the real world apple trees were beginning to disappear. Many of the old Kentish orchards had been turned over to the more profitable production of hops for the burgeoning beer industry, and as a result, the apples sold at market tended to be small, blemished, jumbled up and unnamed, produced mainly in mixed farms or market gardens whose keepers could afford very little of the studied care applied by the gardeners of the gentry.

In stark contrast, apples shipped from abroad were

increasingly appealing. In the USA, where fruit growing benefited from endless space, scientific methods, commercial savvy and, through the American Pomological Society, strong organisation, vast resources were thrown at the production and export of a small portfolio of brightly coloured fruits whose visual appeal more than compensated for any paucity of flavour. By the 1870s, Yankies, as they were known, were being sold by costermongers across the length and breadth of Britain. Canada, too, got in on the act in a big way.

It wasn't until the Royal Horticultural Society finally began to focus on the coarse subject of commerce, freeing itself from the obsessions of the country house set, that a concerted effort was made to organise and promote English apple growers. In 1883, the RHS organised an Apple Congress at its Great Vinery at Chiswick – an incredible gathering of the tribes. Before the show, the committee viewed, identified and logged a staggering 1,545 varieties of British apple and set about trying to unravel the Gordian knot of synonyms that led to the same variety being known by different names in different parts of the country (and possibly in different parts of the same hamlet). Based on a questionnaire, the Congress published a list of the sixty best dessert apples and sixty best cooking apples, with the aim that growers would focus their efforts on the most worthy varieties. The winner in the dessert category was the King of Pippins – anything less would have been embarrassing – and in second place was the Cox's Orange Pippin, a newcomer grown from a seed planted by Richard Cox, a retired brewer in Slough. In the decades that followed, English orcharding soared back into prominence, with the Cox increasingly dominant.

British growers tended to focus on early eating apples, which could be picked before foreign arrivals flooded in, and cooking apples, which no other country – unsteeped as they were in a culture of puddings and pies – bothered to produce. As the great British pomologist Edward Bunyard put it: 'The best English apples by long training know how to behave in a pie; they melt but do not squelch; they inform but do not predominate.' The most famous of these emerged around 1810, when a resident of a modest cottage in Southwell, Nottinghamshire – probably Mary Anne Brailsford – planted some apple pips in its rear garden, producing a tree laden with unusually large and flavour-some fruit. In the 1850s, a young apple enthusiast called Henry Merryweather asked the cottage's then-owner, Matthew Bramley, for permission to take a cutting, and it was in the homeowner's honour that the fruit would be named: Bramley's Seedling. After winning a prestigious certificate at the 1883 Congress, the Bramley caught the attention of commercial growers and quickly started to corner the market.

The decades that followed the RHS Congress saw a significant revival in the quality of English apples. *The Anatomy of Dessert* (1929), Bunyard's beautiful survey of British fruit, essayed almost a full year of extraordinary apples: the Gladstones of late July; the Irish Peach, whose 'fresh acidity with slight spicy aroma accords well with the warm August days'; the arrival in November of the beloved Cox, the 'Chateau Yquem of apples'; December's Blenheim Orange ('The man who cannot appreciate a Blenheim has not come to years of gustatory discretion; he probably drinks sparkling Muscatelle,') and the similarly refined

Orleans Reinette, 'whose brown-red flush and glowing gold do very easily suggest that if Rembrandt had painted a fruit piece he would have chosen this apple'; the misnamed May Queen, which came in January, 'crisp and crackling, with a savour of nuts or almost of the earth'; the late winter apples of February and March, which too often appear like the 'aged and wrinkled harridans who till the Continental fields,' but if properly handled can display 'the plump turgescence of youth'; the season finally ending in early summer with the likes of the Rosemary Russet, 'an aristocrat in every way'.

'It is evident,' wrote Bunyard, 'that each nation has the fruits that it deserves.' Where we are now, then, would make him weep for the country's soul. As Britain revelled in a glorious diversity of apples, other countries were focused on producing a small number of highly consistent, attractive, but slightly humdrum varieties, and as the twentieth century unfolded, it was these varieties – Granny Smith (from Australia), Golden Delicious (from the USA, then France), Gala and Braeburn (both from New Zealand) – that offered the output and homogeneity demanded by the supermarket system. The UK, for all the riches of its historic apple culture, now imports three-quarters of its apples, and many once-famous natives have all but vanished. Even the Blenheim, described by Bunyard less than a century ago as 'one of the best known of our apples,' its renown outstripping that of the palace that shares its name, is rarely seen today. Thanks to global production and controlled atmosphere storage, which keeps fruit in a state of suspended animation, supermarkets can sell the same ten or so international apple varieties all year round, while the rest struggle to find a home beyond organic produce boxes and specialist food markets like Borough.

So, while the apple is still one of our pre-eminent fruits, the romance has all but gone, killed by globalisation and industrial production. Had the forbidden fruit been something tired and grainy, or crudely sugary, picked thousands of miles from Eden and shipped across the world, there's a chance the mother of mankind would have been sufficiently unimpressed to turn it down.

TOMATOES

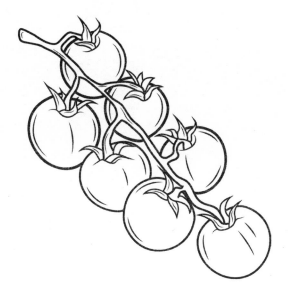

JOHN GERARD, ONE OF ENGLAND'S foremost botanists, had, through extensive reading and personal experience, come to understand the nature of the tomato – and it really wasn't good. In 1597, having sourced the seeds of this weird new fruit from Spain and Italy and planted them in his botanical garden in Holborn, Gerard had some first-hand knowledge that he wanted to share. 'The whole plant is of rank and stinking savour,' he warned. Only those savage types found in 'hot regions' might be willing to eat its berries, and any nourishment they yielded would be 'naught and corrupt'. While he was happy to grow them in his garden, no tomato would ever darken the Gerard salad bowl.

In this, Gerard was far from alone. Many of his continental contemporaries were equally convinced that, while it might make for an attractive ornamental plant, the tomato had absolutely no place in the kitchen. How they came to this conclusion, and why for more than two hundred years much of Europe was needlessly deprived of tangy soups, sauces and salads, tells us a great deal about the prism through which our forebears viewed food.

*   *   *

Wild tomatoes – a family of tiny-fruited plants, meagre in population and narrow in geographic spread – originated in the coastal highlands of Chile, Peru and Ecuador and were probably domesticated on a local scale by Andean farmers. But the fruits whose distant descendants would end up lubricating our sandwiches were first cultivated further north, in the Puebla–Veracruz area of Mexico, their seeds having landed there by happenstance or design. The variety known colloquially as the cherry tomato – which can still be found growing untamed in Mexico and Central America – is the most likely link between the scrawny wild tomatoes of the Andes and our much plumper cultivated forms.

When the tribes known collectively as the Aztecs began settling in the Valley of Mexico from the beginning of the fourteenth century, the tomato was already well established in the region, and they appear to have fallen quickly for its culinary charms. In this, they were aided by their deep-rooted affection for the far more established tomatillo, a yellow or pale green fruit from the same botanical family, which comes wrapped in a dry husk that splits open as the fruit matures, but is otherwise similar to the tomato in its appearance and application. Both were described by the Aztecs using the word *tomatl* – the Nahuatl term for something round and plump – but with different prefixes applied: the tomatillo was *miltomatl*, the tomato *xitomatl*.

Different cultivars followed the same naming pattern. In his *Natural History of New Spain* (1615), Francisco Hernández – the Spanish royal physician who spent much of the 1570s living in Mexico – described the *coatomatl* ('serpent tomatl'), probably a tomato, as 'beautiful, a little bit bigger than nuts; they are green and later they turn yellow'. The *yzhoatomatl*, clearly a tomatillo, was 'larger than almonds, but smaller than walnuts and . . . encased in a skin like a bladder. They go through stages from green to yellow or purple.' The *coztomatl*, yellow in colour and 'covered with certain small bladders,' apparently 'dries up milk' when applied to women's breasts. The Spanish Franciscan friar and pioneering ethnographer Bernardino de Sahagún wrote of traders in the central market of Tenochtitlan, the largest Aztec city, selling 'large tomatls, small tomatls, leaf tomatls, thin tomatls, sweet tomatls, large serpent tomatls, nipple-shaped tomatls, serpent tomatls. He also sells coyote tomatls, sand tomatls, those which are yellow, very yellow, quite yellow, red, very red, quite ruddy, ruddy, bright red, reddish, rosy dawn coloured.'

Faced with this confusing diversity of fruits, the Spanish, who invaded Mexico in 1519 and in a little over two years conquered the Aztec empire, took the easy route linguistically. Rather than creating an individual name for each, they learnt the generic suffix and just ran with that. The Nahuatl tomatl became the Spanish *tomate*, be it a tomato or a tomatillo, whatever its size, colour or similarity to a nipple. When tomatoes and tomatillos began appearing in European gardens in the mid-sixteenth century, it was still rare for any real distinction to be made between them. The Florentine aristocrat Giovanvettorio Soderini wrote an agricultural treatise in the 1590s that gave the two plants individual entries, evident from the accompanying drawings, but even he called them both by the same name. Not that this muddle really mattered, as the tomatillo would soon disappear from view in Europe. It's not entirely clear why, although one enjoyable theory is that the ripe tomatillo's split husk appeared a touch too labial for prudish Catholic sensibilities.

In Mexico, most tomatl fruits were prepared with the use of special bowls whose incised interiors ground the flesh into a coarse salsa, ready to be flavoured with chilli and salt – a preparation still fundamental to Mexican cuisine. Bernal Díaz del Castillo, a soldier who served in the brutal invading army of Hernán Cortés then later told of his adventures in the compelling but not entirely truthful *True History of the Conquest of New Spain* (1576), described how the natives of the town of Cholulla planned to use this salsa as a side dish to a meal whose purpose, he claimed, reflected a wilful misunderstanding of the Europeans' benign intentions. 'They wished to murder us, and eat our flesh,' he wrote, 'for which purpose they had already prepared the dishes, the salt, the pepper, and the tomates.' Incidentally, quite a lot of murdering did end up being done in Cholulla while the Spanish were there, but none of it by the Aztec and with no tasty side dishes made available to share.

Very few of the early European chroniclers of Mexico leave us with the sense that they ever actually ate a tomato – the Jesuit priest José de Acosta, who sang its praises as both a raw food and the base for a sauce, being a rare exception. Francisco Hernández – a doctor, not a gastronome – wrote purely about its health benefits, deeming it 'effective' when rubbed on the body and efficacious in the treatment of blocked tear ducts, stomach aches, mumps, throat inflammation and 'excessive menstrual flow'. And, he wrote, 'mixed with chicken dung and applied with a wick, it is an excellent remedy for sinusitis'. Untreated sinusitis might, on reflection, be preferable.

After the tomato crossed the Atlantic in the sixteenth century, its possible impact on bodily health continued to be a major focus for Europeans who commented upon its arrival. But not many of the notices were even a fraction as positive as Hernández's. Much of what we know about the tomato's early cultivation in Europe can be found in the writings of the continent's burgeoning community of herbalists, and their responses to this strangest of fruits were almost uniformly wary.

Renaissance herbalists were the clean-eating bloggers of their day – similarly influential and factually haphazard but with more of a penchant for learned classical references and fewer sublimated eating disorders. While demonstrating a sharp eye for observation, they were often blinkered by their reverence for the great naturalists and medics of antiquity – writers such as Hippocrates, Dioscorides and Galen – whose view of the natural world they considered gospel. This left them incapable of exploring the new plants arriving from Asia and the Americas in a way that wasn't shaped by the ancients. Convinced of the omniscience of their classical forefathers, herbalists would scour the great texts of natural history to find clues as to the nature of these freakish arrivals. Might the tomato be Dioscorides' glaucium, they asked, or Galen's lycopsericon ('wolf's peach')? Could it be the golden apple from the Garden of the Hesperides? Might it be related to the mandrake, the magical and aphrodisiac powers of which were expounded upon by everyone from Greek natural philosophers to the writers of the Old Testament? All of these names would be used to describe the tomato, as would 'love apple' – possibly a nod to the mythical properties of the mandrake, or perhaps even a nod to those lewd tomatillo husks.

The earliest substantial reference to the tomato's presence in Europe was penned by the Italian herbalist Pietro Andrea Mattioli in his *Discorsi* (1544), a commentary on an ancient Greek pharmacopoeia compiled by Dioscorides. In a chapter on the mandrake, Mattioli suggested that this exotic new fruit, which he deemed it unnecessary to name, was a new species of aubergine – itself a fairly recent arrival, having migrated from Asia following the Arab invasions of Spain and Sicily. He wrote: 'Another species has been brought to Italy in our time, flattened like the *mele rose* [a variety of apple] and segmented, green at first and when ripe of a golden colour.' It was 'eaten in the same manner' as the aubergine: fried in oil and seasoned with salt and pepper.

Ten years later, in a revision to his book, Mattioli alighted upon a name: *pomo d'oro*, meaning 'golden apple', later established in Italian as *pomodoro*. That same year, 1554, the Flemish physician Rembert Dodoens published both a woodcut picture of a tomato and a stark warning to anyone thinking that Mattioli's fried, seasoned tomato slices sounded nice: 'This is a strange plant and not found in this country except in the gardens of some herbalists, where it is sown . . . the complexion, nature and working of this plant is not yet known, but by that I can gather of the taste, it should be cold of nature, especially in the leaves, somewhat like unto the mandrake, and therefore also it is dangerous to be used.' Herbalists were rarely shy of plagiarism, so the words of Mattioli and Dodoens would be repeated all over Europe for decades to come by writers who claimed this important wisdom as their own. Time and again, reference would be made to Italians eating tomatoes, fried and seasoned like aubergines or mushrooms, and to the fruits being extremely cold in nature and offering very little nourishment (those silly Italians!).

According to the enduring Galenic theory of 'humours' – a philosophy formulated in ancient Greece and Rome and named after Galen, a second-century Greco-Roman physician – all plants offered a blend of four inherent 'qualities': hot, cold, moist and dry. Eating them could be either beneficial or dangerous, depending upon the current state of your body's four humours (blood, yellow bile, black bile and phlegm), an imbalance of which would lead inevitably to illness. Tomatoes were deemed to be moist and extremely cold – according to Gerard, 'perhaps in the highest degree of coldness' – which could be highly problematic. The consumption of a cold, moist food would, it was believed, be likely to result in a dangerous excess of phlegm, particularly in cold, damp countries like this one, where people were considered naturally phlegmatic and hot-bloodedness was rare.

As a result, most writers deemed the tomato to be corruptive. In England, a book from 1600 warned that 'the fruit being eaten provoketh loathing and vomiting,' a result more commonly associated today with the late-night doner kebab. The Venetian botanist Pietro Antonio Michiel insisted that a tomato's smell alone could cause eye diseases and headaches, while the physician Giovanni Domenico Sala, writing in 1628, called them 'strange and horrible things' that only 'a few unwise people' were willing to eat. Humours aside, this reticence is easy to understand. Tomatoes were both foreign – although contemporary writers were highly confused as to their origins: Peru? India? Spain? – and odd. They didn't look or taste like anything a European had seen before, and they probably didn't taste anything like as good as they do now, after centuries of selective breeding. Their association with the aubergine didn't help – known as the *mala insana* ('mad apple'), the aubergine was, wrote Michiel, 'harmful to the head,' so being categorised alongside it was far from a compliment. Plus, the leaves and stems have an unusually strong smell – the 'rank and stinking savour' described by Gerard – and are indeed mildly toxic. Applied externally, the juice of the tomato was thought to be effective for the treatment of scabies or burns, but when it came to using the fruit for food, the consensus was solid: steer clear.

Largely because it was known in some places as the love apple (*pomme d'amour* in French), it is often stated that the tomato was considered an aphrodisiac – and some herbals of the time do allude to this reputation – but there is little evidence of this having had any practical consequences (indeed, 'cold' foods were considered passion killers, not a source of ardour). No one was eating tomatoes in the hope of a night of passion. In fact, people weren't even eating them in the hope of a nice salad. Across most of Europe, the tomato grew widely in botanical gardens but rarely found its way into the kitchen.

Italy and Spain, though, were different – southern Italy, in particular, where people were traditionally less averse to the consumption of vegetables than, for example, the meat-obsessed English, who considered plants the lowest form of sustenance. The influence of Spain, which ruled the kingdoms of Naples, Sicily and Sardinia for a large part of the early modern period, was also marked, making the region fertile ground – in every sense – for the Spanish conquistadores' New World discoveries. By the end of the seventeenth century, Antonio Latini, chef to a noble household in Naples, was happily using tomatoes in the palace kitchen without any concern for the resulting levels of phlegm production or passion suppression. Latini's famous book, *Lo Scalco alla Moderna*, published in the 1690s, included a sauce of tomato, chilli, thyme, salt, oil and vinegar, a dish of sautéed aubergine, onion, squash and tomato, and 'cassuola di pomadoro', in which roasted tomatoes were added to a stew of pigeon, veal, chicken necks, herbs, eggs and lemon juice. Oh, and for real savoury depth, some testicles. Two of Latini's recipes referred to the tomato as being of the 'Spanish style' – an indication that the use of this fruit still felt a little foreign, even in its new heartland.

It was in the works of another Neapolitan chef, writing around a century later, that southern Italian cuisine could be seen to be truly taking the tomato to its bosom. Vincenzo Corrado's famous book *Il Cuoco Galante* (1773) began to define a type of cooking now inexorably linked with the Mediterranean – simple and balanced, packed with olive oil and vegetables. The tomato featured heavily, and in very recognisable ways: a tomato soup, topped with basil, thyme and parsley; a tomato sauce flavoured with chilli, garlic, pennyroyal and rue; a dish of whole baked tomatoes stuffed with anchovies, garlic and herbs and topped with golden breadcrumbs. This latter dish Corrado called 'pomidori alla Napolitana' ('Neapolitan-style tomatoes') – by then, no mention of Spain was required.

Spain had been the first port of call for the tomato plant on its long journey to European ubiquity, but at first, its fruit made very little impression on the historical record beyond a few dull lines of household admin and some mundane still-life paintings. Slowly and with very little fanfare, though, the tomato would become an important part of the Iberian diet, particularly in the south. In his *Flora Espanola* (1784), the Spanish botanist José Quer y Martínez described how tomatoes were 'cultivated in great abundance on the truck farms and irrigated fields in all the provinces and lands of our peninsula,' and explained that in the south they could be enjoyed almost all year round, so early did their fruiting begin. Quer wrote of their use as a light breakfast for the field workers of La Mancha and Valencia and as a supper dish of the poor, 'who get fat and strong in the tomato season,' but he also waxed lyrical about their use in 'sumptuous and delicate dishes' enjoyed by the rich, 'seasoning the most delightful foods and forming a delicious sauce'. He dismissed the health concerns expressed by 'those in the north', noting that 'the experience in our peninsula' showed such worries to be baseless: 'Certainly in Spain they are not harmful and are used by the rich and the poor, and neither the former who eat them because they like them nor the latter who eat them out of necessity have suffered the slightest detriment to their health.'

Gradually, the appeal of the tomato spread northwards, to northern Italy and southern France. 'One also begins to find in Lombardy a fruit that is common in Rome, and which is slightly known in Paris,' wrote one late-eighteenth century French visitor to Italy, while a French dictionary of agriculture from 1789 proclaimed: 'In Italy, in Spain, in Provence, and in Languedoc, the fruit of the tomato is very much sought after.' Of any loathing or vomiting, not a mention was made.

For a while, the Brits remained stubbornly unimpressed. In 1673, the English naturalist John Ray, who travelled widely in Italy, included the 'love apple' in a list of the 'many fruits they [Italians] eat, which either we have not, or eat not in England,' – these also included the aubergine and carob, which, according to Ray, the English considered 'fitter meat for swine than men'. Demonstrating just how alien the tomato remained, an English dictionary of 'difficult terms', published in 1677, described the 'love apple' as 'a Spanish root of a colour near violet'. Other than it not really being Spanish, or a root, or violet, this was extremely useful information.

Eliza Smith's hugely popular *The Compleat Housewife* (1727) contained no mention of tomatoes, while Hannah Glasse, another pioneer of English cookery writing, included tomatoes in just one of her hundreds of recipes. Published in 1758 and entitled 'to dress haddocks the Spanish way', this involved cooking the fish with spices, garlic, vinegar and 'some love apples, when in season'. And yet, just a few decades later, the 1797 edition of the *Encyclopaedia Britannica* stated: 'The tomato is in daily use, being either boiled in soups or broths, or served up boiled as garnishes to flesh and meats.' As the fruit became more widely dispersed – and the dodgy foundations of classical medicine became increasingly undermined by the progress of science – the dam was finally breaking.

In 1837, a new edition of *The Cook and Housewife's Manual*, written by the Scottish journalist and novelist Christian Isobel Johnstone under the pseudonym Margaret Dods, included a short addition to the chapter on vegetables and roots, which hadn't been present in her original 1826 version. It stated of tomatoes: 'These have gone down in France, but are just (like other fashions) coming into vogue among us. Tomatas are used both in sauces and soup, and pickled.' Eight years later, Eliza Acton's masterpiece of Victorian food writing *Modern Cookery* (1845) came stacked full of tomato-based recipes, the quantity and breezy nature of which reflected a fruit whose use would by now be far from unsettling to readers.

Acton recorded two recipes for tomato sauce – one 'common', one 'finer' – which she listed among the 'appropriate tureen sauces' for beef steaks, broiled oxtail and 'all roasts of pork, except a sucking pig'. She added tomatoes to curries, roasted them (an excellent garnish for leg of mutton, she suggested), stewed them, and turned them into a creamy puree to be served with meat. She provided two recipes for 'forced tomatas' – stuffed tomatoes – one English, one French, the English one suitably plain and modest (a stuffing of tomato pulp, bread and butter and some optional mushrooms), the French one involving a far more elaborate merging of ingredients, including ham, breadcrumbs and egg yolk. Oh, and for that authentic Gallic edge, garlic, which, Acton warned, 'if added at all, should be parboiled first, as its strong flavour, combined with that of the eschalots, would scarcely suit the general taste'. Tomatoes may have become an acceptable foodstuff, but some foreign flavours remained firmly beyond the pale.

Acton's tomato 'salade' – 'merely sliced, and dressed like cucumbers, with salt, pepper, oil, and vinegar' – was identified in her copy as being in the 'American style'. She also reproduced an American recipe for 'tomata dumplings', copied from an 1842 edition of a US agricultural journal, which involved skinning tomatoes then enveloping them with dough to make dumplings, a method the original writer claimed would enhance 'the delicate spicy flavour which even in their uncooked state makes them such decided favourites with the epicure'. Acton, though, suggested that English tomatoes might not be quite up to the job: 'It is possible that the tomata, which is, we know, abundantly grown and served in a great variety of forms in America, may there, either from a difference of climate, or from some advantages of culture, be produced in greater perfection than with us, and possess really "the delicate spicy flavour" attributed to it in our receipt, but which we cannot say we have ever yet discovered here.'

Spicy or not, tomatoes had by Eliza Acton's time become one of the defining components of the American diet. William Salmon, an English herbalist who from around 1687 spent several years in the American colonies, wrote of seeing tomatoes in the Carolinas. Where the plants came from is not certain – perhaps brought by the Spanish to their settlements in Florida, perhaps through English or French Huguenot migration, or perhaps shipped from the Caribbean, where they'd been cultivated since the sixteenth century – but the introduction of tomato cookery to the Deep South was probably led by black slaves trafficked from the British West Indies. If so, their use would soon cross racial lines and spread gradually northwards. Although American cookbooks remained for a while tightly bound to European culinary traditions, often to the point of straightforward plagiarism, the prominence afforded to tomatoes by the early-nineteenth century pioneers of US cookery writing (the likes of Mary Randolph, Lydia Maria Child and Eliza Leslie) and the novel uses to which they were put – stewed with okra, added to gumbo and chowder, turned into sweet jellies – represented an early divergence between the tastes of the New World and the Old.

The tomato's standing in early-nineteenth century American cooking was inspired at least in part by a complete reversal of the arguments that had for so long hindered its adoption on this side of the Atlantic. In the 1830s, Dr John Cook Bennett, a mediocre academic but first-rate self-publicist, led a campaign to promote the fruit as a medical panacea. His suggestion that the tomato could 'supersede the use of calomel' – a common but entirely ineffectual medicine – in 'the cure of diseases' inspired pharmaceuticals manufacturers to begin selling tomato pills as a remedy for everything from scrofula and syphilis to liver complaints and dyspepsia. This wave of positive publicity did much for the image of the tomato while doing absolutely nothing for the unfortunate syphilis sufferers of America.

Among the most appealing aspects of the tomato is the ease with which it can be preserved, and this quality soon coalesced with the American aptitude for commercial innovation. Americans were not the first to make long-lasting tomato products – an anonymous Sardinian document from the mid-eighteenth century included a recipe for a tart condiment of unripe tomatoes, chillies, sour grapes and vinegar, and by the 1790s, the kitchens of the Saluzzo family in Calabria were making use of a dense, concentrated tomato paste, known as *conserva di pomodoro* – but it was they who turned preserved tomatoes into common household fare. In 1847, New Jersey businessman Harrison Crosby mastered a technique for preserving tomatoes in tins, samples of which he sent to President Polk and Queen Victoria, as well as several newspaper editors. After two years, the *New-York*

Daily Tribune prised open one of Crosby's tins and declared: 'They taste as they would have tasted when plucked from the vine.' Of Queen Victoria's response, amused or otherwise, we know not. Within a decade or two, as the canning process became more refined and reliable, the production of tinned tomatoes had become big business in the United States and the idea was being picked up by European industrialists, thus transforming a whole raft of popular dishes from seasonal specialities into year-round staples.

Today, the defining US foodstuff is tomato ketchup – a product whose roots are found in Asia but whose ubiquity was very much made in America. Inspired by fermented soy and fish sauces, known in the Amoy Chinese dialect as *kê-chiap*, the earliest English ketchup recipes tended to be based upon mushrooms, fish, shellfish or walnuts, all of which emulated that Asian umami hit. The United States took the concept of ketchup – essentially, a bottled sauce used as a condiment – and moved their beloved tomato to its heart, and from the start of the nineteenth century, barely a single American cookbook was published that didn't contain at least one tomato ketchup recipe. In 1876, a Pittsburgh man named Henry J Heinz began mass-producing ketchup, which, to prevent it from spoiling, contained more sugar and vinegar than was usual in most domestic versions. That sweet, sticky, industrially produced gloop would, along with Hollywood and rock 'n' roll, become a key part of the twentieth-century incursion of US culture into every corner of the world – a replay of the tomato's original transit from North America, but one that would prove far more rapidly successful than the first.

In Britain, an enthusiastic adopter of American ketchup,

the average person today consumes more than twenty kilos of tomatoes and tomato products every year – less than half the amount eaten in the United States and way behind the likes of Egypt and Turkey but far from inconsiderable – and the place of the fresh tomato in our diet is no longer restricted even by the seasons. As a result of careful selection and the widespread use of polytunnels, ripening gases and international fulfilment networks, the tomato has become a year-round staple, never absent from the grocery aisles of supermarkets and widely enjoyed despite the insipid nature of a sun-starved fruit that has been picked early and transported hundreds of miles.

At the heart of the tomato's appeal is its remarkable versatility – very few items of produce are equally delicious raw, cooked or preserved, but the tomato pulls its weight in every possible state. In her *Book of Household Management* (1861), Mrs Beeton wrote: 'The more the community becomes acquainted with the many agreeable forms in which the fruit can be prepared, the more widely will its cultivation be extended.' She wasn't wrong. It is impossible now to imagine a Europe without tomato soups, sauces and pickles; without pasta al pomodoro, ratatouille, gazpacho or the cheese and tomato sandwich. And more striking yet to think that just four hundred years ago, John Gerard, despite his ownership of several tomato plants, could never have countenanced eating any one of them.

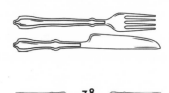

OLIVE OIL

R ISING ABOVE THE TESTACCIO DISTRICT of Rome, a traditionally working-class neighbourhood known for its glass-roofed food market and lively nightlife, is what looks from a distance like a fairly mundane hill, incongruously situated within an otherwise flat landscape, yet far from eye-catching. This, though, is no ordinary landform. Known as Monte Testaccio, it is contrived not from earth and stones but from the pulverised remains of tens of millions of ancient olive oil amphorae.

Completed around 250 CE but dating back several centuries, the Testaccio rubbish heap's construction was a systematic operation typical of an imperial state at the height of its powers. The massive oil-filled amphorae were shipped from around the empire to the nearby Horrea Galbae warehouses to be emptied of their unctuous cargo, before being smashed into manageable pieces and layered up in a tight series of terraces. Most were globular seventy-litre vessels of a style unique to Hispania Baetica, the Roman province in what is now Andalusia, southern Spain; millions more have been traced back to Byzacena (roughly Tunisia) and Tripolitania (Libya).

Monte Testaccio doesn't just offer an insight into ancient

Rome's organised approach to waste disposal; it also attests to its citizens' bottomless appetite for olive oil and the huge quantities that had to be produced on all sides of the Mediterranean in order to feed it. Olive oil was to that corner of the ancient world as petroleum has become to the world at large: economies were built upon it, trade was fuelled by it, great fortunes were made from it, powerful political dynasties rose from it, foreign policy decisions were informed by it, politicians were corrupted by it, and atrocities both terrible and mundane, from enslavement to egregious mislabelling, were committed in its name. There have always been oil regimes. Only the palatability of the oil has changed.

Oleasters – wild olive trees – grow in abundance throughout the lands that skirt the Mediterranean (although a large proportion today are the descendants of previously domesticated plants left to go feral), and these were being exploited for their wood, fruit and oil long before – and long after – the farmers of the Fertile Crescent first began selectively propagating olive groves. The coastal stretches of Syria, Lebanon and Israel are often cited as the likely crucible for this process of domestication – probably in the Chalcolithic period, which began at the end of the fifth millennium BCE, when the people of the region began experimenting with metal tools and organising themselves into complex social structures. At Gilat, in the Negev Desert of southern Israel, among the remains found at a religious sanctuary constructed during this period were numerous torpedo-shaped jars sent from settlements far and wide, which appear to have been used in ritual activities; examination of the organic residues found in these containers identified olive oil as their likely contents.

Wherever the process began, it spread quickly – and for good reason. Olives, like apples, produce offspring very different to their parents when grown from seed, but by planting cuttings from those trees with the most desirable characteristics (sophisticated techniques such as grafting were not required), generations of farmers gradually transformed the small, hard, fiercely bitter fruits of the oleaster into fat, oil-rich olives, carried on smaller plants with less foliage and heavier yields. As a result, the Levant gained access not just to a high grade of salad dressing, but to a fuel and lubricant of exceptional usefulness, provided by a plant that with a little care can aspire to immortality – an olive tree in Ano Vouves, Crete, branches of which were used to make victory wreaths at the 2004 Athens Olympics, is estimated to be at least two thousand years old, and it's still fruiting.

The growing scale of olive production throughout the Bronze and Iron Ages can be deduced from the attempts by cuneiform-scribbling bureaucrats to track and control it. In Ebla, northern Syria, tablets dating from around the twenty-fourth century BCE attested to a large-scale trade in olive oil and the existence of administrators whose role it was to combat the fraudulent cutting of olive oil with cheaper, lower-quality lipids – a problem that persists to this day. In Babylon, the *Code of Hammurabi*, a set of laws carved onto a spectacular black stone stele in the eighteenth century BCE, included among some fairly harsh applications of justice (lots of limbs being sliced off, lots of executions) was the gentler requirement that a merchant transporting olive oil via an agent should expect a receipt.

From the eastern Mediterranean, knowledge of olive cultivation spread westwards, fuelled by the trading and colonising exploits of the Phoenicians, whose Levantine homeland was drenched in olive oil and whose cultural and culinary influence extended to north Africa, southern Spain and just about every island along the way. One of these islands, Crete, got in on the act quite early (whether by the diffusion of plants from the Levant or an entirely independent domestication of native oleasters is an open question), and by the second millennium BCE was shipping oil-filled amphorae far beyond its shores – remnants of these have been uncovered in Egypt, an oil-hungry nation with environmental conditions unfavourable to the production of olives. Olive oil played a major part in the blossoming of Minoan and Mycenaean Crete, attested to by the unremitting quantity and vast scale of pithoi jars uncovered in the mighty palace of Knossos, and just about every other nook and cranny of the island.

The next great envoys of the olive were the Greeks, who began colonising the Mediterranean in the eighth century BCE. It was they who took domesticated olives to southern Italy, Sicily and Sardinia, and it was through contact with the Greek colonies that Etruscans carried cuttings to the rest of Italy, establishing another major centre of diversification. A Greek settlement also flourished in Provence, southern France, a region that retains a very un-Gallic preference for oil over butter.

To any ancient Athenian, the idea that the olive's story had begun in the Levant would have sounded like utter madness. The olive tree 'is a thing such as I have not heard of on Asian ground, nor as ever yet born in the great Dorian isle of Pelops,' wrote Sophocles, completely erroneously, convinced as all his compatriots were that Athens was its true birthing place. According to the city's foundation myth, when King Cecrops of Attica established his new capital, the gods Poseidon and Athena each presented its citizens with a gift: Poseidon, a saltwater spring; Athena, an olive tree. With the invention of the saline drip still some way off, the Atticans decided that Athena's tree was a more useful endowment than Poseidon's undrinkable water, so the goddess was made patron of the city that now bears her name. Her tree supposedly lives on in the grounds of the Acropolis, having miraculously survived the destruction wrought by the invading Persian army in 480 BCE. According to Herodotus: 'It happened that the olive tree was burnt by the barbarians with the rest of the sacred precinct, but on the day after its burning, when the Athenians ordered by the king to sacrifice went up to the sacred precinct, they saw a shoot of about a cubit's length sprung from the stump.'

Sacred olive trees purportedly cut from Athena's gift could be found scattered around the Athenian territories. Aristotle wrote of how the farmers on whose lands they grew were each year expected to provide the state with the oil rendered from their hallowed fruit, some of which was used to reward the winning gymnasts and jockeys at the Panathenaic Games. At one stage, he wrote, cutting down a sacred tree was even punishable by death. Ordinary olive plantations, too, were protected by law. Demosthenes, a contemporary of Aristotle, explained that, for the sake of future generations, anyone who dug up more than two olive trees in a year would be forced to pay the state 100 drachmae per tree, plus the same amount to whoever had grassed them up.

As well as being a food, olive oil was used throughout the ancient world as a fuel for lamps and furnaces, as a lubricant, as a medicine, and as a base for perfumes and body lotions. Israel was a major producer of scented oils – one of the Hebrew Psalms listed among the divine gifts bestowed upon humanity 'wine that maketh glad the heart of man, and oil to make his face to shine,' – as were Cyprus and Crete, thanks to the Mediterranean islands' stunning array of herbs and flowers. Classical Greece, though, took the use of unguents to a whole new level. At the bathhouses, gyms and stadia, no self-respecting athlete would dream of bathing or exercising without first being slathered head to toe in perfumed olive oil. The residue of this oil, collected from sweaty patrons' skin, was sold as a remedy: Pliny the Elder, who found the whole concept pretty disgusting, wrote of how 'scrapings from the bodies of athletes' were used by the Greeks to treat 'contractions of the uterus' and 'inflammations of the rectum', among other conditions. A similar medicament was made from oil retrieved from walls, floors, baths and statues. According to the first-century Greek physician Dioscorides, oily grime from the wrestling school was good for the joints, while grime from the gymnasium was better for 'abrasions, the removal of scaliness, and old ulcers'.

As with so many aspects of Hellenic culture, the Romans took what the Greeks had done, stripped away some of its romance, and increased its scale many times over. It was Roman horticulturalists who left the first detailed instructions for the management of olive plantations, which abounded throughout the Italian peninsula, but Italy alone couldn't produce enough oil – particularly after Septimius Severus, who rose from olive oil wealth in north Africa to become emperor of Rome, added oil to the 'annona': the free food parcels distributed to poorer citizens. To meet the city's needs, the empire was thoroughly rinsed for oil. After the Libyan city of Leptis Magna made the mistake of supporting the wrong side in the Roman civil war, the victorious Julius Caesar demanded an annual tribute of three million pounds of olive oil, a crippling quantity, while Andalusia, the source of much of the Monte Testaccio rubble, was used as a massive olive oil sweatshop – a precursor to the transformation of Europe's American colonies into slave-powered factories for coffee and su BCE gar.

In 77–79 CE, Pliny described fifteen varieties of olives sourced from around the empire, distinguishing between those that were good for eating and those that were good for oil. His suggestion of where the best oils came from was fairly predictable: 'In the production of this blessing . . . Italy holds the highest rank among all countries.' Like many of his countrymen, he praised the oil of Venafro, in the central Italian region of Molise: 'It is our unguents which have brought this oil into such great esteem, the peculiar odour of it adapting itself so well to the full development of their qualities; at the same time its delicate flavour equally enlists the palate in its behalf.' Marcus Terentius Varro, writing a century or so earlier, included Venafro's oil in a list of his homeland's great foods: 'What spelt shall I compare to the Campanian, what wheat to the Apulian, what wine to the Falernian, what oil to the Venafran?'

Oil from Liburnia, now part of Croatia, was also highly

valued, as can be inferred from an ancient piece of dupery. In *De Re Coquinaria*, a first-century Roman recipe collection, a suggestion was made for how inferior Spanish oil could be passed off as the primo Liburnian stuff through the addition of powdered elecampane, Cyprian rush and green laurel. 'Sift this in and add finely ground salt and stir industriously for three days or more. Then allow to settle. Everybody will take this for Liburnian oil.'

The method of production was understood by the ancients to be fundamental to the quality of the resulting oil. 'The first oil of all, produced from the raw olive before it has begun to ripen, is considered preferable to all the others in flavour,' Pliny explained. 'In this kind, too, the first droppings of the press are the most esteemed, diminishing gradually in goodness and value . . . The riper the berry, the more unctuous the juice, and the less agreeable the taste.' In 301 CE, a set of price controls issued by Emperor Diocletian defined three classes of olive oil – 'floris', derived from the word for flower, but used to mean something in its perfect state; 'sequentis', the second pressing; and 'cibari', meaning ordinary or common – with the first of these being just over three times the price of the cheap stuff.

According to *The Geoponica*, a collection of agricultural lore produced in tenth-century Constantinople but compiled from much older Greek and Roman sources, other more surprising factors could also impact on quality. 'The olive being pure, ought to have them that gather it chaste; and they ought to swear that they come from their own wife's, not from another's bed, for it will thus produce a great abundance of fruit for the time to come,' it suggested. 'They say also, that in Anarzarbe of Cilicia [southern Anatolia], chaste boys cultivate the olive, and for this reason, that the olive is there very fruitful.' The same tract offered the helpful suggestion that if a mouse, or any other animal, has fallen into your olive oil, the 'unsavoury smell' from its corpse could be removed with the addition of coriander seed, dried fenugreek or red hot coals of burnt olive wood.

The Romans regularly shipped olive oil to far-flung corners of the empire, including Britain – an island with plenty of mice but no olive oil for them to fall into. Thousands of amphorae, mostly Spanish but some north African, have been uncovered in cities such as London and Colchester and in the heavily militarised area by Hadrian's Wall – wherever Roman troops were stationed, olive oil followed. Freighting all those heavy jars to this cold, distant realm must have been an expensive and logistically challenging business, but while legionaries became inured to Britain's grim weather and savage locals, they clearly couldn't cope without their favourite fat.

That brief interlude aside, Britain would remain a land fried in lard and lubricated by butter. But even after the Romans left, small amounts of olive oil continued to make their way into the kitchens of the wealthy. The royal cookbook *The Forme of Cury* (c.1390) included a handful of mentions of 'oyle de olyf'. The instructions for 'porrey chapeleyn' – basically, battered onion rings – required 'an hundred onyons' to be halved, cooked in 'oyle de olyf and almond milk, separated into rings, lightly battered, then fried again in either more olive oil or 'wyte grees', the former of which definitely sounds more appealing. Another recipe suggested olive oil as an alternative to beef broth as a medium in which to cook apples – an option it specified as being for 'fysch dayes'.

This reference was a telling one. On fish days – the Catholic days of fasting – the liberal use of olive oil was perfectly acceptable, while butter and other animal fats were outlawed unless permission had been purchased through a payment to the Church. In those northern European regions that lacked olive oil of their own, it was a source of some resentment that the clergy, the seat of whose power lay in Rome in the heart of olive country, were not just upholding this rather unfair rule but directly profiting from it. As Martin Luther put it: 'At Rome they themselves laugh at the fasts, making us foreigners eat the oil with which they would not grease their shoes, and afterwards selling us liberty to eat butter.'

After England became a Protestant country and could happily gorge on butter every day of the week, the next putative invaders of these islands took similar preparatory measures to those of the Romans fifteen centuries earlier. When the Spanish Armada set off in 1588, its ships were provisioned with more than eleven thousand arrobas of olive oil (around forty thousand gallons) – over a gallon per soldier, designed to last through a six-month stint on this olive-free isle. King Philip II may have misjudged completely the speed of his enemy's fleet and the malevolence of our storms, but he fully understood the British ambivalence towards any fat that didn't come from an animal.

That ambivalence, though, only fully extended to olive oil's use in the kitchen. For centuries, producers of olive oil found Britain to be a useful dumping ground for the worst dregs of their output, convinced as we were that this golden unguent was a medicine, not a food. Pharmacies abounded with the stuff. In *Pharmacopoeia Bateana*, a collection of the prescriptions of the seventeenth-century court physician George Bate, olive oil was used in dozens of potions. One remedy, good against 'pustules of the lips, and cancers of the breasts,' instructed the chemist to take live toads and 'boil them in oil-olive for one hour, or till they break; then strain and keep it for use'. A similar recipe using live frogs could, it was stated, be used against 'redness of the face' as well as gangrene and cancer (usefully, though, William Salmon, who edited the 1694 edition of the book, noted in his commentary that toad-infused olive oil was a much more effective medicine).

Britain did eat some, but not much. As Mrs Beeton explained in 1861: 'The oil extracted from olives, called olive oil, or salad oil, is, with the continentals, in continual request, more dishes being prepared with than without it, we should imagine.' The British, on the other hand, occasionally drizzled it onto lettuce in the hope they might fart less: 'With us, it is principally used in mixing a salad, and when thus employed, it tends to prevent fermentation, and is an antidote against flatulency.' Any olive oil that could be bought in Britain was generally vile. 'Really good pure olive oil is almost unknown outside the boundaries of Italy,' wrote Nathaniel Newnham Davis in *The Gourmet's Guide to Europe* (1903). 'An Italian gentleman never eats salad when travelling in foreign countries, for his palate, used to the finest oils, revolts against the liquid fit only for the lubrication of machinery he so often is offered in Germany, England, and France.'

In the middle of the twentieth century, Elizabeth David's evangelism for olive oil had a profound influence on the British – or at least on the kind of British people who read Elizabeth David – but access remained an issue. Writing in 1963, she noted that good Italian oil could then be bought 'in Soho, but almost nowhere else' and that 'anything marked simply "salad oil" is best left alone'. Pharmacies remained the principal stockists. The chef Simon Hopkinson recalled in his cookbook *Roast Chicken and Other Stories* (1994): 'The first time I made mayonnaise, the olive oil I used came from Boots the chemist. It was a small bottle, pretty tasteless and quite clearly not meant for culinary purposes.'

It wasn't until the 1990s that things began to change, as foreign holidays, cholesterol scares and the sight of a young Jamie Oliver chucking it around with gleeful abandon drove olive oil into the public consciousness. In 1991, the UK got through six thousand eight hundred tonnes of olive oil; by 2018 we were pouring and drizzling just short of ten times that amount (although, to put that in perspective, Italy, with a slightly smaller population, consistently gets through well over half a million tonnes a year). Britain's enthusiastic embrace of olive oil was indicative of a wider surge in global demand through the twentieth century, which did little to change where oil was being made – Spain is by a country mile the world's biggest producer, still fulfilling the role imposed two thousand years ago by its Roman conquerors, followed by Italy and Greece, with Turkey, Tunisia and Morocco close behind – but did have a significant impact on its character. Olive oil became big business, and fortunes were waiting to be made from its rapid transformation into an industrial product.

For thousands of years, almost all olive oil was produced in the manner described by the ancients, using grindstones and presses, but the application of science and technology changed everything, with mixed results. Some producers adopted modern techniques for crushing, malaxing (mixing the olive paste) and centrifuging (spinning the paste to separate out the oil) while still insisting on the highest standards, but the international market also began to heave with heavily refined oils made from rancid, overripe olives, whose unpleasant odours and flavours had to be treated with heat and chemicals to make them palatable.

In 1960, a series of helpful categories were introduced throughout Europe, defined by their production methods, chemical composition and taste. At the top of the list came extra virgin oil. Guided by the International Olive Council (an intergovernmental organisation, which, in a nice nod to those oil-soaked Greek athletes, carries the same initials as the International Olympic Committee and faces similar accusations of being dangerously beholden to commercial interests), the rules that govern what can and cannot be sold as extra virgin have been enshrined in EU law since 1991. At first sight, they seem strict: to take the name, an oil must have acidity and peroxide levels below a set limit, and when tasted must be both identifiably fruity and completely flawless, with not the slightest hint of anything rancid or musty. The problem is that without extensive testing, such criteria are rendered meaningless, meaning that a lot of muck currently sells for an awful lot of brass – campaigners for stricter regulation insist that were the legally defined taste test more rigorously applied, the vast majority of mass-produced extra virgin oils would fail.

There is nothing wrong with cheap oil – should you wish to grease a pan for some sausages or coat your naked body before tossing a discus, an industrially produced olive oil might well do the job. The problem is that flawed oil is frequently mis-sold as extra virgin, and even the most industrially refined oils, if mixed with a tiny bit of extra virgin, are – perfectly legally – sold as 'olive oil' and promoted as being 'pure' and 'light', profiting from the vestigial sense of healthful naturalness that clings to the name, despite having been chemically stripped of all flavour and nutritional value.

Today, if what you want is a real extra virgin olive oil to dress your salad and address your flatulence – oil that belts out a harmonic song of fruitiness, bitterness and pepperiness – the best thing to do is buy it from the people who made it, or from people who know the people who made it. Ask them about the olive variety, the production method and the local weather. Ask them about the oil's character. Ask them for a taste. Just don't ask them about the chastity of the pickers. That hypothesis remains unproven.

COFFEE

S URPRISINGLY, GIVEN HOW THOROUGHLY THE liquor of its roasted beans now soaks the daily life of the planet, coffee is something of a newcomer. Compared with beer, wine and tea, whose stories are woven into the histories of the world's oldest civilisations, the drink that wakes up the planet each morning is a brash arriviste – a market disruptor that conquered the world like a tech giant, changing everything for better or worse. Often worse.

The *Coffea arabica* plant first worked its magic in the highlands of Ethiopia, where its bright red, stimulant-packed cherries were consumed by local tribespeople. European writers of the seventeenth century liked to attribute the discovery of the plant's vivifying qualities to an Ethiopian herder who, inspired by the remarkable friskiness of his sheep or goats, ate the fruit on which the flock had been grazing and then, hyped up on caffeine, vigorously set about spreading the word. A fun story, but, as is the case with so many fun stories, almost certainly not a true one.

At some unrecorded juncture, coffee plants established themselves across the Red Sea on the Arabian Peninsula. It was in Yemen that a drink made by brewing the grounds of roasted beans first emerged, and it was the mystics of the region's Sufi religious orders who proved to be the architects of its burgeoning popularity. Adherents of Sufism, a form of Islamic mysticism, seek to shed themselves of worldly concerns and commune more closely with the divine, and one route to achieving this spiritual congress is the 'dhikr': a ritual that aims, often through the rhythmic repetition of recitation, song or movement, to concentrate the mind on the presence of God. As dhikrs often took place in the dead of night, when a trance-like state can easily tip into a deep, unenlightening sleep, the discovery of coffee proved revelatory. It is, of course, possible that rural Yemenis had been quietly quaffing hot coffee for centuries without choosing to share it with the world, but it was the Sufi orders, which included an abundance of cosmopolitan, well-travelled men, that took the beverage abroad, caused it to be written about for the first time and began its close – if occasionally fractious – association with Islam.

The most illuminating account of coffee's rapid diffusion was produced in the 1550s by Abd al-Qadir al-Jaziri, a writer based in Cairo. Quoting the words of an earlier authority, Ibn Abd al-Ghaffar, Jaziri described how 'qahwa' had been used in Yemen 'by Sufi shaykhs and others to help them stay awake during their devotional exercises'; a Sufi imam known as Dhabhani, who died around 1470, was, he suggested, responsible for the drink's 'emergence and spread'. By the last decade of the fifteenth century, coffee had made its way from Yemen to Mecca, and by the first decade of the sixteenth century had arrived in Egypt, where it was used to stimulate nocturnal worship in the 'Yemeni quarters' of Cairo's vast al-Azhar mosque complex. Here, Jaziri wrote, the Sufis 'drank it every Monday and

Friday evening, putting it in a large vessel made of red clay. Their leader ladled it out with a small dipper and gave it to them to drink, passing it to the right while they recited one of their usual formulas, mostly "there is no god but God, the master, the clear reality".' Before long, coffee was being sold in the streets around the mosque and was moving into the city's secular realm. The same transition soon happened throughout the territories of the Mamluk Sultanate, which ruled over Egypt and the Hejaz. In no time at all, the coffeehouse had become a defining institution of Arab social intercourse.

Coffee's rapid progress was not without controversy, with some Islamic jurists suggesting it should, like alcohol, be considered *haram* – forbidden. Whether or not coffee counted as *khamr* – a word that in its narrowest definition meant fermented grape juice, but was generally interpreted as referring to any intoxicating substance – was, as the drink took a grip on Arab society, a source of some debate. The suggestion that coffee should be proscribed on religious grounds upset many devout, coffee-loving writers, whose response was summed up in a passage attributed to the Egyptian scholar Suyuti: 'One drinks coffee with the name of the Lord on his lips, and stays awake, while the person who seeks wanton delight in intoxicants disregards the Lord, and gets drunk.' This interpretation tended to prevail, but coffee's social and religious acceptability remained precarious.

In 1511, the governor of Mecca, Kha'ir Beg, banned the sale of coffee, his argument being that the gatherings it inspired were morally undesirable and that the drink itself was bad for health. Coffee beans were burned in the streets (an act of state violence that at least would have smelt good), and many vendors and drinkers were beaten up. A letter was dispatched by the governor's legal team to the authorities in Cairo requesting that a general prohibition be enforced throughout the Mamluk lands, but the response came back that, while the carousing prompted by its consumption was indeed a concern, there was nothing fundamentally wrong with the drink itself. Fifteen years later, another attempt was made to close the coffeehouses of Mecca, but this too fizzled out.

A pattern was set: coffee was accepted as righteous, but the same could not be said of the establishments in which it was drunk. Opposition came from religious conservatives who argued (with some justification) that coffeehouses were dens of iniquity, rife with gambling, prostitution and ribald conversation. Skittish secular authorities, meanwhile, were wary of the political threat posed by the communal consumption of an energising drink. After the Ottoman Empire subsumed the Mamluk Sultanate in 1517 and coffee-house culture was disseminated across the empire's vast territories, bans were sporadically enforced by the autocrats of Istanbul. According to the Ottoman scholar Kâtip Çelebi, writing in the 1650s, 'coffeehouses experienced varying fortunes for several years, now banned, now permitted'.

The most prolonged period of prohibition began in 1633 when the public consumption of coffee in Istanbul was made a capital crime by the uncompromising Ottoman sultan Murad IV. Spooked by the fate of his predecessor Osman II, who had been murdered in a military coup, Murad was eager to snuff out the slightest threat of rebellion and coffeehouses were, he believed, the dark corners in which an insurgency would be fomented. About twenty years after the ban began, Çelebi wrote of how the coffeehouses of the capital were still 'as desolate as the hearts of the ignorant'. Those outside the city had, though, continued to flourish, and before long Istanbul was back to being, as it remains, a place where coffee and conversation could be obtained several times over on every street. Throughout its history, the success of coffee has – like that of alcohol, pornography and Frankie Goes to Hollywood – provided persistent affirmation that when enough people get a kick from consuming something, official proscription will ultimately prove futile.

The first westerner to write about coffee was Leonhard Rauwolf, a German physician, who described a visit to Aleppo, Syria in 1573: 'They have a very good drink, by them called "chaube", that is almost as black as ink, and very good in illness, chiefly that of the stomach; of this they drink in the morning early in open places before everybody, without any fear or regard, out of china cups, as hot as they can.' This kicked off a sudden surge of European accounts, including in 1601 the first by an Englishman, William Parry. Writing about his adventures in the Islamic world alongside the charismatic Elizabethan gadabout Antony Sherley, Parry described 'a certaine liquor, which they do call coffe, which is made of seede much like mustard seede, which will soone intoxicate the braine like our metheglin'. Given that metheglin is distinctly alcoholic and coffee quite clearly isn't, it seems dubious that he actually tried this exotic brew – but had he done so it's unlikely he would have enjoyed it much. Certainly, the other Englishmen who encountered it on their travels weren't exactly glowing in their reviews. In 1610, the poet Sir George Sandys described Turkish coffee as 'blacke as soote, and tasting not much unlike it'.

Its initial oddness to the English palate did not, however, inhibit the swift assimilation of a drink whose alluring exoticism appealed to the country's more cosmopolitan citizens. The first reliable record of coffee being drunk in England came in a May 1637 diary entry by the naturalist John Evelyn, who mentioned it being consumed at Baliol College, Oxford, by one Nathaniel Conopios. Much of Evelyn's diary was collated later in his life, and it's likely that his dating was askew by at least a year: according to one of his Oxford contemporaries, the historian Anthony Wood, Conopios was a Greek Orthodox cleric who fled to England from Istanbul in 1638 after his boss, Cyril Lucaris, patriarch of Constantinople, was strangled at the behest of the Ottoman sultan. Wood did, however, concur with Evelyn as to the refugee's choice of breakfast brew: 'He made the drink for his own use called coffey, and usually drank it every morning, being the first, as the ancients of that house have informed me, that was ever drank in Oxon.'

Wood also made mention of what may have been Britain's first coffeehouse. Referring to the year 1650 (or possibly 1651), he wrote: 'This yeare Jacob a Jew opened a coffey house at the Angel in the parish of St Peter, in the East Oxon; and there it was by some, who delighted in noveltie, drank.' Not long afterwards, in 1652, Londoners – notorious, then as now, for delighting in novelty – were confronted by their first sight of a coffeehouse (described by one chronicler as a 'shed'), which appeared within the tight warren of alleyways behind St Michael Cornhill in the City of London and was at least part-owned by another enterprising immigrant, Pasqua Rosée. Originally from Ragusa (modern-day Dubrovnik), but living in Smyrna, then part of the coffee-drenched Ottoman Empire, Rosée was taken into the employment of a British merchant, Daniel Edwards, who brought him back to London and introduced him to a city as yet unawakened to the thrill of a coffee buzz. Having established his coffeehouse, the Ragusan's marketing message was strong: one handbill suggested that as well as preventing drowsiness (plausibly enough), coffee's 'vertues' included protection against consumption, coughs, dropsy, gout, scurvy, scrofula, miscarriages and the deeply unpleasant-sounding 'hypocondriack winds'.

Such hyperbolic claims were a common feature of European descriptions of coffee. Muslim medics had tended to agree that coffee was, under the Galenic system of medicine, cold and dry in nature (something of a leap for the modern drinker, who would consider hotness and wetness to be its primary characteristics). While this represented a danger for anyone with a melancholic disposition, and could also undermine sexual potency, Arab physicians noted that coffee had plenty of beneficial effects. These were dramatically amplified by European writers, who – much like today – liked to wildly sensationalise the virtues and dangers of anything new or foreign. Soon, the kind of hysterically positive notices exemplified by Rosée's handbill were being countered by similarly overstated warnings of terrible side-effects. In Marseilles in 1679, as part of a coordinated academic assault on the growing French appetite for coffee, a doctor called Claude Colomb publicly decried the 'general exhaustion, paralysis and impotence' that would result from its consumption. Colomb also presented the beautifully Gallic objection that coffee had 'tended almost completely to disaccustom people from the enjoyment of wine' – an unforgivable state of affairs.

For the most part, as coffeehouse culture took hold in Europe's cities, these medical naysayers were roundly ignored – particularly in London. Here, the social scene would be utterly transformed by the buzzing crowds who took this miraculous new beverage to their hearts. In the words of one appalled poet, coffee (a 'Turkish renegade') seduced the English 'snap by snap, / As hungry Dogs, do scalding porrige lap'. By May 1663, there were eighty-two coffeehouses operating within the tight confines of the Square Mile, with dozens more springing up around Covent Garden. Contemporary estimates from the first half of the eighteenth century suggested that thousands of coffee shops were in operation in London. Nowhere else in the world – not even Istanbul – could claim such an extraordinary concentration of cafes.

It is hard to overstate the importance of the coffeehouse on the commercial and political life of Restoration England, providing as it did a place for men (and it was largely just men) to gather, talk and make deals while being marginally less drunk than usual. Many of the activities now associated with investment banking, share trading and insurance evolved in London's cafes – the insurance market Lloyd's of London started life in Lloyd's Coffeehouse on Tower Street, a popular haunt for merchants and ship-owners. The nascent newspaper industry was also sparked into life by demand for information and entertainment from these bustling pits of caffeinated interaction.

Different political factions all had their favourite haunts. Thomas d'Urfey's comic play *Sir Barnaby Whigg* (1681) drew a laugh with the line: 'In a coffeehouse, just now among the rabble, I bluntly asked, which is the treason table?' But Charles II wasn't laughing. In December 1675, the King, whose father had been beheaded just a couple of decades previously and who, like Murad IV, had an understandable aversion to sedition, published a proclamation banning coffeehouses, insisting that from their smoky rooms 'diverse false, malicious and scandalous reports are devised and spread abroad'. Such was the public outcry, though, the ban was quickly withdrawn.

A more entertaining objection to coffeehouses was presented in 1674 in the form of *The Women's Petition Against Coffee*. In this pamphlet – often cited as though it made a serious contribution to the debate, despite clearly being composed as a smutty satire – the almost audibly smirking writer complained that London's men were being rendered impotent by the coffeehouse ('they come from it with nothing moist but their snotty noses, nothing stiff but their joints, nor standing but their ears') and that, far from being a sobering influence, coffee was being used as fuel for even heavier drinking ('like tennis balls between two rackets, the fopps our husbands are bandied to and fro all day between the coffeehouse and tavern').

The drink these foppish husbands were consuming was not a refined one. Since emerging in Arabia, coffee had been brewed using a decoction method, with the grounds boiled up in a pot over a stove or fire – an approach still favoured in much of Turkey, North Africa and the Middle East, but which unless executed with skill, care and well-prepared beans can result in a gritty, bitter drink. During the London coffee boom, some coffeehouses used isinglass – a substance obtained from the dried swim bladders of fish, also used to clarify beer – to clean up the murk. Still, smooth it was not. The addition of milk, which covers a multitude of sins, took several centuries to catch on both in Europe and the Islamic world – the sixteenth-century Syrian-Arab physician Dawud al-Antaki warned that 'some drink it with milk, but it is an error, and such as may bring in danger of the leprosy' – and for the most part coffee was drunk black and, until sugar became more widely available, unsweetened.

The French were the great innovators of less muddy preparations. The idea of infusing coffee into hot water through a cloth bag emerged in the early eighteenth century. Around a hundred years later, the De Belloy pot – a vessel consisting of two stacked chambers, divided by a metal filter on which the grounds would rest, allowing the infused water to drip through – pioneered the percolation method, also known as the French drip. French inventors would spend most of the nineteenth century patenting increasingly clever, beautiful and often pointlessly elaborate percolators, filters and infusers, all of which helped to address the grittiness of old-style boiled coffee, but without being particularly efficient.

In 1884, Angelo Moriondo, a hotel owner from Turin, Italy, was granted a patent for 'new steam machinery for the economic and instantaneous confection of coffee beverage'. By using a capacious boiler to force pressurised steam through a large bed of coffee, Moriondo sought to speed up the bulk production of the drink. His idea, which he refined over the years without ever making any money, was developed by Luigi Bezzerra, who in 1901 patented a version that dispensed the steam-propelled coffee directly into a single cup. And thus the espresso was born. By 1906, the first commercial espresso machines – gorgeous, decorative, metallic contraptions – were being produced under the La Pavoni brand.

After the Second World War, Milanese coffee shop owner Achille Gaggia built a lever-operated espresso machine that utilised pressurised water rather than steam, resulting in a less bitter coffee topped with a foamy 'crema'. Gaggia's compact, chrome-plated machines cemented espresso as the very essence of stylish modernity and in the decades that followed, Italian migrants took this aspirational new style of coffee to the streets of London and New York. Since the 1990s, espresso-based drinks have come to dominate British and American coffee culture (with, in recent years, significant input from Australia and New Zealand, inventors of the long black and flat white), as well as continuing to underpin the daily existence of most Italian people, for whom *un caffè* means 'an espresso', with no ambiguity whatsoever.

As brewing methods were shifting, so too was the supply of coffee. At the start of the European coffee boom, almost all the world's beans were grown in the drink's historic homeland of Yemen and exported from the port of Mocha – a monopoly jealously guarded by Yemen's Ottoman overlords and then, after a rebellion had seen off the Turks in 1634, by its native Zaidi rulers. The British East India Company fought to wrest control of the European side of the Mocha trade, and the resulting profits helped fuel Britain's colonising activities elsewhere. The Dutch, whose previous dominance of Asian trade had been superseded by the British, decided to seek a different route to profits. Starting in 1696, the Dutch East India Company made a concerted effort to establish its own coffee plantations on the Indonesian island of Java. The success of Javanese coffee, the first sales of which took place in 1711, sparked a rush by European powers to introduce the crop to their slave-powered colonies in the Caribbean and the Americas. What had for centuries been purely an Arabian product rapidly became a global one – a change that dealt a devastating blow to the once-booming economy of Yemen.

Britain toyed with coffee cultivation in its New World colonies, but when it came to the grim exploitation of American land and African people, its cash crops of choice were more often sugar, tobacco and cotton. In the eighteenth century, as the influence of Britain on the supply and pricing of coffee began to fade, Chinese tea – an import over which the British maintained a far greater level of commercial control – became the metropolitan drink of choice, and it was only really in the late twentieth century that coffee drinking began to regain the popularity and status it had enjoyed in the first century or two after its arrival in London.

Meanwhile, the rest of the planet's consumption grew unabated, bolstered by the hearty appetite for coffee that developed in the United States. By the end of the nineteenth century, the USA was consuming almost half the world's crop. To keep pace with demand, more and more equatorial land around the globe was seeded with coffee plants – by 1750, coffee was being grown on five continents – but this explosion in cultivation came at an awful human and environmental cost. In 1773, the French botanist Jacques-Henri Bernardin de Saint-Pierre observed: 'I do not know if coffee and sugar are essential to the happiness of Europe, but I know well that these two products have accounted for the unhappiness of two great regions of the world: America has been depopulated so as to have land on which to plant them; Africa has been depopulated so as to have the people to cultivate them.'

Even as European colonial power in the Americas began to shrink, coffee production remained gruesomely exploitative. In 1822, Brazil declared independence from Portugal and rapidly turned itself into the world's biggest coffee producer, but the nation's economic rise was powered by the labour of millions of slaves and the destruction of vast swathes of virgin forest. Brazil's reliance on unpaid servitude, and the world's reliance on Brazil to feed its coffee habit, resulted in the country's abolition of slavery lagging behind every other nation in the western hemisphere. It was only in 1888 that all slaves were emancipated, and then only because a new – and more economical – form of exploitation had filled the void: poor European workers, mainly from Italy, shipped across the Atlantic, then forced to pay off the plantation owners for the cost of their crossing. As a result, freedom did little to improve the lives of black Brazilians, with racist bosses preferring to employ white migrants, who were considered genetically superior but still eminently exploitable.

In the second half of the nineteenth century, political leaders in Central America began to see coffee as the perfect crop with which to enrich their nations and themselves, and the impact was similarly grim, even without the use of African slaves. The usual pattern was for productive farmland to be requisitioned by the government, then sold off cheaply to wealthy families or – particularly in Guatemala – European migrants, while the indigenous people who had tended that land for centuries were chased away at gunpoint. Once the coffee fincas were established, those same indigenous people – their traditional livelihoods now destroyed – were coerced into selling their labour to the plantation owners on terms not far removed from slavery.

Life on a colonial coffee plantation in East Asia was no picnic either. James Thurber, a nineteenth-century American writer and former coffee dealer, described 'the contempt and want of consideration with which the natives are treated' in the Dutch colony of Java, where the authorities 'maintained a most grinding despotism over their miserable subjects, levying forced loans and otherwise despoiling those who, by exceptional industry and prudence, have accumulated anything beyond their daily subsistence'. Workers on the plantations overseen by the British in India and Sri Lanka were, it hardly need be said, kept similarly poor and oppressed, while the profits from Asian coffee production flowed relentlessly westwards.

Until suddenly they weren't flowing quite so freely. In 1869, a deadly fungus began to spread through Sri Lanka, causing a condition known as 'coffee leaf rust'. Within a few years, the coffee industry of the East Indies was all but wiped out. This disaster prompted the sudden rise to prominence of a sub-Saharan African coffee species, *Coffea canephora* – 'discovered' by Europeans in the late nineteenth century, but already widely enjoyed by Africans. Branded 'robusta', its beans are harsh and highly caffeinated, but the plants proved hardy and rust-resistant. Introduced by Asian producers to regenerate their decimated plantations, robusta's suitability for use in instant coffee (a product launched on a large scale in the USA in 1910 and popularised by Nescafé after 1938) has seen its share of the global market rocket to beyond forty per cent, with Vietnam the largest source by far. Throughout Africa, the continent that spawned both main species, coffee exports are now a major source of income. Uganda, Kenya and Tanzania have built significant coffee industries and in Ethiopia, where this whole story started, native arabica varieties – some of exceptional quality – are far and away the country's most valuable crop.

As coffee increased its grip on American households in the nineteenth century, high demand, fluctuating supply and the possibility of either huge profits or damaging losses made it a product ripe for commoditisation in the pulsing new heartland of capitalism. After a coffee price bubble burst in 1880, ruining many in the industry, a coffee exchange was incorporated in New York in 1881, and speculators rushed in, bringing the benefits of commercial liquidity and access to investment, but also making the market increasingly complex, faceless and iniquitous. 'Coffee is the most speculative business in the world,' pronounced the American coffee magnate John Arbuckle in 1897, and that remains not far from the truth today.

The global coffee trade is still as murky as a seventeenth-century stove-boiled decoction. Markets for coffee – like those of other soft commodities such as cocoa and sugar – are a regular target for high-frequency traders, whose decisions are based on computer algorithms that react to, and hence create, second-by-second price movements, rather than being shaped by studied analysis of supply and demand. The price of coffee has, as a result, become wildly volatile and increasingly detached from the real world of growers, roasters, baristas and consumers. The economic bounty from the world's staggering capacity for cappuccinos is largely enjoyed by hedge funds, middlemen, global food corporations and tax-averse coffee shop chains, while those who cultivate the beans in the fields of Brazil, Colombia, Vietnam and Ethiopia remain poorly rewarded, their live-lihoods at the mercy of economic forces far beyond their control. Large parts of the developing world have become hostage to an unstable monoculture, the price for which can collapse in a heartbeat, thanks to the machinations of the markets – little wonder that poverty, political instability and the presence of powerful drug cartels remain such prevalent features of many coffee-producing nations. For centuries, authorities in the Middle East, Turkey and western Europe worried about the potential of the coffeehouse to cause social and political mayhem. They seemingly had a point – but rather than the places where coffee is drunk, it is the places where coffee is grown that too often feel the sting.

Such are the iniquities of the system, it is now incumbent upon any coffee drinker with a conscience to seek out beans that have passed along the shortest of supply chains, from producers who've been fairly remunerated for their skill and hard work. Thankfully, the recent resurgence of London's vibrant coffee culture, and its subsequent diffusion to other cities and towns, has made that possible. Pioneers like Anita Le Roy, who founded Borough Market's much-loved Monmouth Coffee Company in 1978, drew a clear line between the characterless nature of the anonymous beans pumped out by a rapacious global coffee system and the exploitation of the workers who fed it. The idea that the best cup of coffee is one made from beans of an identifiable variety, produced on a single estate by growers whose knowledge is nurtured and valued, has since been embraced by a growing constituency of ethically minded importers, roasteries, retailers and coffee shops. Good coffee should always have bitter notes. It shouldn't have to leave a bitter taste.

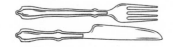

VINEGAR

W HEN IT FIRST ANNOUNCED ITS presence to our prehistoric ancestors, vinegar was less a condiment, more a party-crasher. No one invited it. Very few people were happy when it appeared. But it showed up nonetheless in their casks, jars and wineskins, sour and unpleasant, ruining the fun for everyone. It was only later, on sober reflection, that we would come to appreciate vinegar for what it can be: a vibrant source of balance and punch, rather than a tragic waste of perfectly good booze.

For vinegar to emerge, two natural processes need to play out in sequence: alcoholic fermentation, then acetic fermentation. In the right conditions, yeasts feed on the sugars in vegetables, fruit or cereals and turn them into alcohol – a routine embraced and encouraged by humans since the weightless joy of intoxication was first discovered many millennia ago – but if the resulting liquor is left exposed to the air, a group of common microorganisms known as acetic acid bacteria get to work, triggering a chemical reaction that converts alcohol and oxygen into water and acetic acid: vinegar. The only way to keep these bacteria from making their mischief is to ensure that no oxygen is present. It's no surprise, then, that the invention of the airtight stopper, made from clay or resin, followed on remarkably swiftly from the invention of wine and beer.

Because vinegar is in essence just ruined booze, the forms found in different corners of the world followed in lockstep with the alcoholic drinks consumed there. In China, where rice wine has been drunk for thousands of years, rice vinegars have been produced, deliberately or otherwise, for precisely as long. In *The Rites of Zhou*, a classic work of Confucianism published in the second century BCE but purporting to be from the Western Zhou dynasty many centuries before, an idealised bureaucracy was said to include within its ranks a 'vinegar steward', whose job it was to keep the palace well stocked with what continues to be one of the country's favourite condiments. Japan and Korea, both early adopters of rice as a base for brewing alcohol, followed suit with their production of vinegar, which remains deeply embedded in both cuisines. When winemaking took hold in Assyria, Mesopotamia, Egypt and the Mediterranean, wine vinegar followed. Wine made from dates was used in Babylon, while in Persia, according to the Greek soldier and historian Xenophon, writing around 370 BCE, the available provisions included 'wine of palm, and boiled vinegar from the same source'. In the cold north of Europe, mead, ale and beer provided the foundations.

The hereditary connection between alcohol and vinegar is preserved in the word itself. 'Vinegar', which entered common parlance around the fourteenth century, is derived from the French *vinaigre*. *Vin* is a French word that even British people whose foreign language limits extend only as far as ordering drinks would recognise; *aigre* means 'sour'. In Latin, from which the French language evolved, vinegar was *vinum acre* or *vinum acetum*: sour or acidic wine.

Analysis of vinegar's ancient production and consumption is often rendered more than a little knotty by this intimate association with spoiled drink. There is a clear qualitative difference between a vinegar produced in a controlled way for use in the kitchen and a batch of wine that has turned a bit rough – either through acetic fermentation or one of the other myriad ways that a fermented drink can spoil – but before the processes involved were fully understood, the world's languages often failed to illuminate this distinction. Whether a useful condiment or a barely palatable drink consumed by people who couldn't afford anything better, vinum acetum was just vinum acetum.

A piece of inscribed Egyptian pottery found at the workers' village of Deir el-Medina, close to Luxor, dating from around 1300 BCE, recorded transactions made in the purchase of, among other things, a door, a mat and the services of a magician, all of which were exchanged for what were either large jars of vinegar or, as some historians have suggested, bad wine. (For some, the difference was marginal: Martial, the first-century Roman poet, used one of his epigrams to mock the standard of Egyptian wine-making, proving that Italian culinary snobbery is nothing new. 'Disdain not this amphora of Egyptian vinegar,' he wrote. 'It was much worse when it was wine.') The ancient Greek poet Alexis got to the heart of the matter in a suitably acid-tongued verse about the fussiness and idiocy of people. 'Sour wine we spit out, but go into ecstasies over a vinegar salad,' he moaned. His suggested remedy for this innate hypocrisy was, it must be said, a little drastic: 'Best it is not to be born at all, but if one be born, let him die with all speed.'

A surviving fragment of a fourth-century BCE play called *The Woman Who Left Her Husband* offered confirmation that a salad dressed with vinegar could indeed be ecstatically received by the Greeks: 'For such condiments must speedily rouse the sensory organs of men when they are old, dispel the sloth and bluntness of their desire, and make them glad to eat.' It wasn't just salads either. The food-loving Hellenic poet Archestratus – who lived in Sicily around the same time and became known as 'the Daedalus of tasty dishes' – was an advocate for drenching fish in vinegar, a combination of which any chippy-loving Brit would approve. 'Whensoe'er Orion is setting in the heavens,' he wrote, 'and the mother of the wine-bearing cluster begins to cast away her tresses, then have a baked sarg [white sea bream], overspread with cheese, large, hot, and rent with pungent vinegar, for its flesh is by nature tough. And so be mindful and dress every tough fish in the same way.' Only tough fish, mind you: 'The large she-tunny, whose mother-city is Byzantium,' – better known as the tuna fish – could, said Archestratus, be dipped into a peppery sauce or else eaten entirely unadorned, 'but if you serve it sprinkled with vinegar, it is done for'.

The first-century Roman recipe collection known as *Apicius* or *De Re Coquinaria* provided a vivid insight into rich citizens' diets at the height of the empire. Vinegar appeared on just about every page, and from the breadth and sophistication of the uses to which it was put – as a preservative, a marinade, a dressing or the base of a sauce – it is clear that the bottles and skins found in the cellars of the wealthy weren't filled with spoiled wine but with a carefully crafted and highly valued product. Cooked meat, fried fish, fresh vegetables, even 'hard skinned peaches', were all preserved in vinegar. Raw or cooked vegetables – beets, cucumbers, carrots – came with a simple dressing of vinegar and olive oil, as remains the case on just about every Italian table. There were highly flavoured sour sauces aplenty: mortaria, a little like salsa verde, with crushed green herbs sweetened in honey and sharpened with vinegar; a cumin and vinegar sauce for shellfish; oxygarum, for which herbs and spices were crushed into a paste, bound with honey, then added to vinegar and stock (then later, as the name suggests, often mixed with the fermented fish sauce known as garum). Just about every roast or stew – lamb, wild boar or gazelle, chicken, flamingo or parrot, 'sterile sow's womb' or the magnificently titled 'birds of all kinds that have a goatish smell' – came with a sousing of the old vinum acetum. Moving through the pages of *De Re Coquinaria*, seeing again and again the instruction to 'add vinegar to taste', it's clear that the cheffy instinct to balance sourness and sweetness is as old as the hills.

In ancient Rome, posca – a drink of diluted vinegar (or, more likely, spoiled wine: that old problem again), often infused with herbs – was consumed in large quantities by the common people of the city and in more refined forms by the rich. It also became a regular part of the army's rations – a compilation of laws issued after 313 CE decreed that soldiers on a campaign should receive 'ordinary wine on one day, sour wine on the other'. In his book *Parallel Lives*, the biographer Plutarch used the drinking of posca to illustrate the manly, steadfast character of Cato the Elder, who as a young officer in the Punic Wars shunned the luxuries his status could have afforded him: 'Water was what he drank on his campaigns, except that once in a while, in a raging thirst, he would call for vinegar, or, when his strength was failing, would add a little wine.'

Posca was also the last thing drunk by Jesus. One of the few details of the crucifixion story agreed on by all four gospel writers was the intervention of a Roman soldier who gave him vinegar to drink to ease his suffering on the cross. Drinking vinegar sounds rather unpleasant – and indeed some interpretations of the Bible have erroneously characterised the legionary's generosity as an act of heathen malice – but the benefits of consuming posca, particularly for an army, were notable; certainly, its acidity would have killed some of the harmful bacteria commonly found in water, making upset stomachs less likely.

Ancient medics – and the medieval doctors who followed their lead – waxed lyrical about the health benefits of this acidic liquid. Given vinegar's antiseptic qualities, many of the uses they suggested were quite sensible – for example, Hippocrates, the Greek father of medicine, recommended it for treating head injuries or cleaning ulcers – but others were as misguided as those promoted by today's online peddlers of cider vinegar diets and cures (none of whom have the excuse of being born before the advent of clinical trials). The Roman naturalist Pliny the Elder described twenty-eight remedies that utilised vinegar, tackling everything from nausea and leprous sores to sunstroke and millipede bites. Perhaps the most baffling was that 'retained in the mouth, it prevents a person from being inconvenienced by the heat of the bath'.

Pliny also recorded a famous story about vinegar. Cleopatra, he wrote, insisted to her lover Mark Antony – a man increasingly jaded by everyday excess – that she could arrange a blowout of such opulence that a single entertainment would cost ten million sesterces. The feast appeared at first to be no more insanely lavish than normal, 'magnificent in every respect, though no better than his usual repast'. Then the Queen pulled out her party trick. 'In obedience to her instructions, the servants placed before her a single vessel, which was filled with vinegar, a liquid, the sharpness and strength of which is able to dissolve pearls. At this moment she was wearing in her ears those choicest and most rare and unique productions of nature; and while Antony was waiting to see what she was going to do, taking one of them from out of her ear, she threw it into the vinegar, and directly it was melted, swallowed it.' The bet was won. Suetonius, in *The Twelve Caesars* (121 CE), used a similar story to condemn the 'reckless extravagance' of Emperor Caligula, who, he wrote, 'would drink pearls of great price dissolved in vinegar, and set before his guests loaves and meats of gold, declaring that a man ought either to be frugal or Caesar'. Both stories are almost certainly apocryphal: vinegar of sufficient acidity to dissolve a pearl would be entirely unpalatable even while showing off in an epic way.

Vinegar, unlike the booze from which it is made, has long played a central role in the cuisines of the Islamic world. It certainly came with a hefty seal of approval: in the *Sahih Muslim*, a ninth-century collection of the prophet's sayings, Muhammad was quoted as believing vinegar to be 'the best of condiments'. It continued: 'Abdullah reported that Allah's

Apostle (may peace be upon him) asked his family for condiment. They (the members of his household) said: "We have nothing with us but vinegar". He asked for it, he began to eat it, and then said: "Vinegar is a good condiment, vinegar is a good condiment."' Its chemical properties and medical benefits were studied by Muslim scientists to a significant degree. As early as the eighth century, the great Jabir Ibn Hayyan, alchemist at the court of Caliph Harun al-Rashid, whose understanding of controlled experimentation vastly outstripped that of any European contemporary, wrote at length about vinegar and even achieved the isolation of acetic acid through distillation.

While eschewing much of their complicated science, medieval Europeans enthusiastically embraced the Arabs' interest in alchemy – the seductive but utterly doomed pursuit of lab-manufactured gold – and vinegar was considered an important ingredient by many of its proponents. According to Basilius Valentinus – ostensibly a fifteenth-century German alchemist, but more likely a sixteenth-century writer working pseudonymously – 'in medicine and alchemy, it is impossible to do anything useful without the help of vinegar'. He quite liked it on his dinner as well, though: 'As a seasoning, too, there is no kind that is more agreeable.'

That agreeable seasoning was, by then, being produced on a fairly large scale in the French town that would make its name as the unquestioned home of wine vinegar. Set on the banks of the Loire, within easy reach of Paris, Orléans blossomed as a major staging post on the way from the wine regions of the south to the mansions and palaces of the French capital. A lot of wine passed through this vital inland port, making it a natural location for any dodgy barrels to be repurposed into vinegar. In 1394, a 'corporation' (not unlike an English guild) was established in the city under the snappy name Vinaigriers, Moutardiers, Sauciers, Distillateurs en Eau-de-vie et Esprit-de-vin Buffetiers. In 1580, the corporation's members were formally granted a monopoly on vinegar-making by Henry III, allowing it to grow into a major operation. At its peak in the eighteenth century, there were around three hundred 'vinaigriers' producing vinegar under its (necessarily rather long) banner.

Although the vinegar corporation was disbanded in the aftermath of the French Revolution, when monopolistic privileges were seen as a barrier to progress, the city continued to dominate vinegar manufacturing. The sophisticated method of production that evolved in Orléans (and became known, not particularly imaginatively, as the Orléans process) involved 'mother of vinegar' – a culture of acetic acid bacteria that can be found floating on the top of fermenting vinegar – being continually reutilised, with some of the acidified liquid carefully racked off from beneath it and the same amount of fresh wine funnelled into the barrel to continue the fermentation. Each batch of wine would take about three weeks to turn to vinegar, which was then aged in oak for several months.

The labour-intensive, time-consuming nature of the Orléans process meant that the dominance of the city's artisan vinaigriers would be dangerously imperilled by the development of more economical production methods elsewhere in Europe. In the 1820s, the invention in Germany of the revolutionary Schüzenbach system made fast, high-volume vinegar production a possibility, while the scientific breakthroughs of Johann Wolfgang Döbereiner and Louis Pasteur, who between them identified the chemical reaction that creates vinegar and the bacteria that drive it, hastened the industrialisation of what had once been an esoteric craft. The decline of the traditional vinaigriers was slow but ultimately terminal. Some of the world's finest wine vinegars still utilise the Orléans process, but almost none of them are made in Orléans.

Here in Britain, we didn't produce wine, so we didn't produce much wine vinegar. What we did conjure up in unseemly quantities was ale, so our condiment of choice was by necessity malt vinegar. Wherever there were breweries, there tended to be vinegar makers waiting to give new life to any spoiled barrels. This direct connection between the two industries gradually weakened over time as producers began fermenting the malt themselves, creating an alcoholic base known as 'gyne'. Plenty of space was required to turn gyne into vinegar: needing warmth, the fermenting barrels would be stored outside in the spring and summer, a process known as 'fielding', and stored inside in heated rooms in the autumn and winter, known as 'stoving'. Although the punchy brew that resulted was occasionally described as 'alegar' – an early reference to which can be found in a fourteenth-century recipe for 'noumbles in Lent', bringing sharpness to a dish of fish blood, onions and spices – this somewhat clunky compound word never managed to dislodge its French-inspired antecedent, much to the annoyance of some pedants: the lexicographer Jonathan Boucher complained in 1801 that 'inaccuracy prevails in our common speech, in which the acid liquor, in daily use, whether made of sugar, cyder, ale or wine, is indiscriminately called vinegar'.

Like Boucher himself, some British malt vinegars did have a slightly winey character. John Nott's *The Cooks and Confectioners Dictionary* (1723) provided instructions for a hybrid made using a 'middling sort of beer, indifferently well hopp'd' to which was added mashed 'rapes', the grape mulch left behind from the winemaking process, and by the nineteenth century it wasn't unusual for commercially produced vinegar to be finished in a rape-tun – a special barrel with a false bottom upon which this fruity flavouring could be loaded. Incidentally, Nott also suggested making a kind of pound shop wine vinegar from dried fruit: 'Put spring-water into a vessel, and every gallon, three pound of Malaga raisins, set the vessel in the sun for four months, or till it is safe for us.'

Vinegar was produced in large quantities all over the country, but nowhere more so than in the vicinity of Borough Market, an area with a long history of brewing. Since at least 1641, there had been a 'vinegar yard' on Castle Street – now Thrale Street. In 1790, this was taken over by the Pott family, owners of a similar manufactory on Mansel Street, and expanded into a vast operation – one of the largest in England – covering large swathes of Bankside, next to the similarly gargantuan Barclay Perkins brewery. Other major local manufacturers included Beaufoy, based in Bristol but with a facility in Waterloo, and Vickers & Slee in Bermondsey. North of the Thames, the big competitors were Champions on City Road, and Sarson's, founded in Shoreditch around 1794. The old Vickers & Slee factory on Tower Bridge Road, by then operating under the Sarson's

brand following a complex sequence of mergers and take-
overs, continued producing vinegar until 1992, making it
one of the last of the great Bermondsey food processing
factories to close. Now, almost all malt vinegar brands in
the UK are owned by the same handful of mega-corporations
that own just about everything else.

The most famous of Europe's regional vinegars has bucked
the trend of Orléans and London by continuing to thrive.
Produced in the towns of Modena and Reggio Emilia, in
the Emilia-Romagna region of northern Italy, and made
from the painstakingly slow fermentation of boiled grape
must, balsamic vinegar evolved from the concentrated
grape must syrups known as defrutum and sapa, which
were staples of the Roman kitchen. At some point, the
people of Emilia-Romagna learnt that through a pains-
taking process of very gentle acetification, spread out over
many years, a rich, complex vinegar could emerge from
this treacle.

The first reference to a highly prized vinegar from
Modena – one of sufficient quality to be fed to a Holy
Roman Emperor – came in the twelfth-century poem *Vita
Mathildis*, written by the monk Donizo of Canossa, who
described how in the year 1046 the local lord presented
vinegar as a gift to Henry III. After 1598, the palace of
Cesare d'Este, Duke of Modena and Reggio, had its own
acetaia, where a fine vinegar was produced, and it is in the
records of the Este family that the oldest surviving description of this vinegar as *balsamico* – meaning 'healing' or
'health-giving' – can be found, dating from 1747. Frequent
references to balsamic vinegar only began to emerge in the

nineteenth century, when this beautiful elixir began to be marketed outside the region for the first time.

In 1819, an inventory of the Duke of Modena's storerooms divided the stocks into *balsamico*, *mezzo balsamico* ('half-balsamic'), *fino* ('fine') and *ordinario* ('ordinary'), suggesting a clear hierarchy. Such a hierarchy was formalised in the protected name status introduced after the vinegar's global appeal – and economic importance – rapidly mushroomed in the late twentieth century, leading to a significant diffusion in quality. The far cheaper and less complex 'balsamic vinegar of Modena' can include both wine vinegar and caramel alongside the must, but 'traditional balsamic vinegar' – the real stuff – has to be produced from pure grape must and aged for at least twelve years.

The latter is a condiment of quite staggering beauty, the production of which involves so much more than the intervention of some pesky bacteria. Few things in the culinary world could be further apart than a bottle of traditional balsamic vinegar and a container of badly stored, microbially challenged wine suitable only for a thirsty legionary. Thanks to centuries of human craft, ingenuity and devotion to the taste buds, vinum acetum is no longer always just vinum acetum.

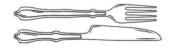

HERRING

I N THE 1790S, AS THE Reign of Terror gripped France and an orchestrated campaign of political violence built to its blood-soaked crescendo, the moderate parliamentarian Bernard Germain de Lacépède decided that being a vocal opponent of political violence was no longer the job for him. Leaving politics behind, he turned his attention to a project far less likely to end in his dismemberment: the production of a five-volume natural history of fish. In it, Lacépède cast his eye over several of the exotic, world-changing foods discussed elsewhere in this book and came to a striking but entirely reasonable conclusion: 'The herring is one of those products, the use of which decides the destiny of empires. The coffee bean, the tea leaf, the spices of the torrid zones . . . all have less influence on the wealth of nations than the herring of the Atlantic ocean. Luxury and caprice demand the former; necessity lays claim to the herring.'

Necessity's interest in this small, bony, world-changing fish was certainly well founded. Packed with vitamins and fatty acids, the herring's rich, gutsy flesh is highly nutritious. More importantly, it is – or certainly was – a foodstuff of quite staggering abundance. As a species, the herring's primary defence against a panoply of predators is to have as many children as possible (the average female produces between ten thousand and sixty thousand eggs) and then coalesce in such numbers that even the hungriest killer whale will struggle to make a dent. Most of their life is spent deep in the ocean, but once a year the shoals, which can cover dozens of square kilometres and contain hundreds of millions of fish, migrate inshore to unleash their heavy payload. Any shoreline whose shallow banks are chosen as a spawning ground will be visited every twelve months by a churning silver tsunami of protein, just begging to be caught.

Given the grinding nature of humanity's daily search for sustenance, the sudden appearance close to land of such a vast and frictionless bounty bordered on the miraculous. On Fridays, saints' days and the forty-day stretch of Lent, Catholic dietary laws meant that meat and dairy were off the menu, and the eating of fish was actively encouraged. Due to its rich oiliness, fresh herring goes off quickly – even now, with reliable refrigeration, it needs to be eaten within a couple of days – but when cured with salt to create a product known generically as 'white herring', it can last for months. Church strictures fuelled an incessant Europe-wide clamour for preserved fish and underpinned a widespread belief that the migration of the herring shoals must be divinely orchestrated. As one eighteenth-century writer put it: 'No reason for their transit can be assigned but the careful hand of God.'

In Britain, God proved even-handed in his favour. Every spring, a wave of herring would roll in off the Outer Hebrides and the north-west coast of Scotland; Orkney and Shetland would be visited in the early summer, followed by Peterhead and the Moray Firth. By late summer, the fish would be appearing near Grimsby and Scarborough, then finally, in the autumn months, in the waters off East Anglia. The fishermen and merchants who followed this clockwise rotation assumed they were pursuing a single mass of fish on an epic chase around the island; what they were actually doing was encountering several distinct population groups, each with different physical characteristics, spawning grounds and reproductive calendars: in every month of the year, at least one population of Atlantic herring will take its turn to spawn.

Wave after wave of settlers learnt to make use of Britain's great aquatic gift. The Romans left behind piles of herring bones in their East Anglian encampments. The Anglo-Saxons were major herring eaters and used the cured fish as a source of revenue and a store of value – the annals of Barking Abbey mentioned the levying of tax called 'herring silver'. The Normans followed suit, and the Domesday Book, compiled in 1086, was littered with examples of rents being paid with salted herring. The village of Beccles in Suffolk paid an annual rent of sixty thousand herring to the Abbey of St Edmund; the nearby port of Dunwich was liable for a total of sixty-eight thousand; and Hugh de Montfort, a Norman noble who was either extremely partial to a fish supper or keen to encourage the development of the local fishing industry, demanded herring rents from his Suffolk estates in quantities both small and massive.

Herring would remain a feature of feudal land grants deep into the medieval period, although their value was sometimes more symbolic than financial: every year, the Norfolk manor of Carleton was obliged to bake for the King twenty-four herring pies, made from the season's first catch, and deliver them 'wheresoever he should be in

England' – an obligation later inherited by the city of Norwich. This duty was still being taken seriously in 1629, when a letter of complaint was sent from Hampton Court to the sheriffs of Norwich decrying the inadequacy of that year's pies, which were tardy in their arrival, stingy with the filling, inadequate in the consistency of the pastry and 'diverse of them also much broken'.

Among the people whose lives were most clearly defined by the North Sea's abundance of herring were the residents of Yarmouth in Norfolk, a port blessed with deep waters, a long natural quay and a favourable position – easily accessible from four rivers that snake inland through East Anglia, and by sea from the Cinque Ports, a medieval confederation of coastal towns on the south-eastern tip of England (Hastings, New Romney, Dover, Hythe and Sandwich), whose fishermen would sail north in search of herring. Through a succession of Norman charters, the Cinque Ports accumulated various powers over Yarmouth, including the right to administer the town's massive annual herring fair, which started on 29th September and lasted for forty days. The role of these southern interlopers became problematic after 1208, when, in recognition of its growing economic importance, the Norfolk town was granted its own somewhat contradictory freedoms and protections by King John. In the century that followed, the two sides were not averse to occasionally arming themselves to the teeth and sailing off to sink each other's ships.

The 1357 Statute of Herring, which set maximum prices for herring sales at Yarmouth and sought to stamp out the profiteering of some of the more aggressively entrepreneurial locals, was just one of a succession of government interventions designed to ensure a steady flow of cheap fish and calm the tensions between rival ports, including a near-perpetual beef between Yarmouth and Lowestoft. The state's interest in herring fishing was deep-seated. After all, there were vital revenues to be had from abroad: the Dutch and French fishing boats that traversed the North Sea had no choice but to land their highly perishable catches on British soil for salting, a privilege for which they were keenly fleeced. England's fishing towns also provided ships and sailors for a near-constant sequence of cross-Channel rumbles – in 1347, when Edward III successfully laid siege to Calais, Yarmouth provided forty-three vessels and over a thousand mariners, and contributed vital supplies of cured herring to feed the troops. In 1429, in what became known as the Battle of Herrings, French forces and their Scottish allies attempted to ambush a massive consignment of 'herring and lenton stuffe' on its way to supply the English army laying siege to Orléans. According to the chronicler Raphael Holinshed, after a 'long and cruell fight, the Englishmen drove backe and vanquished the proud Frenchmen, and compelled them to flee'. The English and their cured fish continued on, unscathed.

The fish pulled from the seas around Britain were highly valued, but their influence on medieval Europe was dwarfed by that of their cousins in the Baltic, from whose fruitful organs the first of Lacépède's herring empires was spawned. In the twelfth century, following a shift in migration patterns, herring began appearing in staggering quantities off Skåne, on the southern tip of Sweden. In *The History of the Danes* (c.1208–1218), the historian Saxo Grammaticus described the seas as containing 'such plentiful shoals that sometimes boats striking them have difficulty in rowing clear and no fishing gear but the hands is needed to take them'. The most significant beneficiaries of this rich seam of silver were not Nordic but German, hailing from the opposite side of the Sound. The emergence of the Skåne fishery coincided with – and dramatically accelerated – the rise of the Hanseatic League, a confederation of German merchant towns with easy access to saltworks (Lüneburg, one of the Hansa towns, was a prolific producer of high-quality salt) and an unparalleled talent for collective bargaining. While allowing Scandinavians to do most of the fishing, the League slowly imposed its grip on the processing, preserving and onward sale of white herring from the Skåne herring market, the profits from which seeded a vast commercial empire. Using lobbying, inducements, blockades, embargoes and – if all else failed – open warfare, the Hansards gained complete control of the lucrative flow of food and raw materials from the Baltic and cloth and manufactured goods from western Europe.

Then, in the fifteenth century, just as suddenly as they had arrived, the fish went away. According to the sixteenth-century Norwegian historian Peder Claussøn Friis, the Skåne fish were said to have 'disappeared by magic, bad men having sunk a copper horse in the sea and thereby driven the herrings away from the coast,' but he himself favoured as a rationale 'the wickedness of men, their abuse of God's good gifts and their godless life'. His was a conclusion rooted in an Old Testament warning about the consequences of swearing, lying, killing, stealing or adultery: 'Therefore shall the land mourn, and every one that dwelleth therein shall languish, with the beasts of the field, and with the fowls of heaven; yea, the fishes of the sea also shall be taken away.' Until recently, when overfishing and changes in climate were pegged as likelier causes of a fishery's sudden failure, poor catches were almost always blamed on a lack of moral rectitude – often with a particular focus on adultery, which had the benefit of forcing much of the blame to be borne by women (a trope cleverly adapted by the menfolk of the Isle of Skye, where according to Samuel Johnson local tradition held that 'if any woman crosses the water to the opposite island, the herrings will desert the coast').

The loss of the Skåne fishery precipitated the slow decline of the Hanseatic League. It also meant that Europe's most abundant source of herring was no longer in the Baltic; it was off the coast of Britain. But as had been the case in Scandinavia, it wasn't the locals whose destiny would be shaped most dramatically by these riches – it was a growing force from across the water.

With great plenty comes inevitable complacency. While the English and Scottish herring ports wallowed contentedly in the natural advantages afforded by their location, fishermen in the Netherlands were driven to innovate. At some point in the fourteenth century, the Dutch discovered that by immediately gutting and cleaning herring before salting them, rather than curing them whole, a far more delicate and reliably preserved product would result – an innovation attributed to a possibly entirely mythical fisherman called Willem Beukelszoon (the one hundred and fifty-seventh greatest Dutchman in history according to a 2005 poll).

The success of the 'Dutch cure' sparked the development of massive fishing boats known as *busses* – expensive to build and hard to manoeuvre, but with holds sufficiently cavernous to allow masses of fish to be gutted and cured straight away without the need to land on British soil. Supported by nippy little jagers, which raced home with barrels of salted fish, and equipped with massive drift nets (another Dutch invention), fleets of busses were able to stay out in the North Sea for months on end, dragging in fish in quantities the English and Scots – outgunned, impotent and increasingly resentful – could only dream of.

Writing in 1607, William Camden despaired at how the 'lazinesse' of the English approach to the herring fisheries had led to the nation 'resigning . . . the profit unto strangers. For it is almost incredible what infinite summes of money the Hollanders raise unto themselves by this their fishing in our shore.' These profits allowed the Netherlands – a collection of tiny, featureless, resource-poor provinces – to construct a merchant navy of intimidating size and sophistication and finance the building of a global empire. First the Dutch controlled the herring trade, then they controlled the spice trade, the tea trade and the coffee trade, and the money kept rolling in. Amsterdam, Europe's new commercial capital, was, the saying went, 'built on herring bones'. England, meanwhile, faced the indignity of having to buy North Sea fish back from the Dutch. As Sir Walter Raleigh put it: 'That any nation should carry away out of this kingdom yearly great masses of money for fish taken in our seas, and sold again by them to us, must needs be a great dishonour to our nation, and hindrance to this realm.'

In the 1530s, the Scottish crown, stung by the Dutch

dominance of its fishery, began sending naval patrols to scare off the busses. When that same Stuart monarchy gained sovereignty over England in 1603, this confrontational stance migrated to London, together with a growing interest in the novel concept of 'territorial waters'. It's no coincidence that it was a Dutch philosopher, Huigh de Groot, who in 1609 gave form to the ancient principle that seas were, like the air, 'common to all'. Nor is it a coincidence that it was an Englishman, John Selden, whose book *Mare Clausum* ('closed waters') set out the more radical counterargument that our sea was our sea and everyone else could just do one. James I, Charles I and Oliver Cromwell all enacted legislation restricting foreign access to British waters and ports, while the Dutch responded by loudly shouting about the inalienable freedom of the seas and providing their busses with seriously well-armed naval escorts to ram the message home. This tension over fishing rights was one of the major causes of the Anglo-Dutch Wars, which began in 1652 and raged intermittently for more than a century. The advantage in these messy conflicts see-sawed back and forth, but it was the Dutch who had the most to lose. With naval engagements and state-sanctioned piracy often making it impossible for the busses to safely enter the North Sea fisheries, other less risky commercial interests began to take precedence in Amsterdam. As the Dutch herring fleet shrank (until the 1650s it numbered some two thousand boats, by 1779 it was down to one hundred and sixty-two), Britannia finally ruled the waves.

This was all very well, but a couple of problems remained. First, British demand for cured fish was not holding up, with the Reformation having seen off the Catholic concept of the fish day. In 1563, alarmed by the unintended impact of Protestantism on the coastal economy, Elizabeth I's government had sought to reinforce the practice of fasting 'for the increase of fishermen and mariners,' adding the slightly Trumpian threat that 'whoever should preach or teach that eating of fish or forbearing of flesh was for the saving of the soul of man, or for the service of God, should be punished as the spreader of false news'. But with many Protestants defiantly ignoring a law that carried about it a strong stench of popery, the decline in demand for cured herring continued unabated.

Even more problematically, nobody else really wanted our herring either. The Dutch had not only pioneered a more subtle method for curing fish, they'd also refined a strict system of regulation that controlled everything from the source of the salt to the minimum quality standard for any fish sent out into the international markets (fall short, and it had to be eaten in the Netherlands). The far less skilled and considerably more laissez-faire Brits produced terrible products and moaned about not being able to sell them. According to one seventeenth-century expert, the main problem with English white herring was that 'the salt is of such an irregular size that the third part of it does not dissolve in proper time,' which led to 'a mortification or kind of rottenness'. And those were the good fish: 'The worser sort or bad ones . . . are deezed over a wood fire, and are thereby dried and rendered red, or red-herrings.'

The red herring was a whole fish, heavily salted and then cold-smoked for days on end until stiff as a board – and it was famously vile. About the only person with anything good to say about this East Anglian classic was the Elizabethan writer Thomas Nash, whose magnificently odd *Nashes Lenten Stuffe, or The Prayse of the Red Herring,* (1599) combined elaborate denigration of Catholics with even more elaborate praise of Yarmouth's signature product. Nash, though, was not being entirely serious. 'I had money lent me at Yarmouth,' he wrote in the book's introduction, 'and I pay them again in praise of their town and the red herring.' Far more tellingly, the biggest importers of British red herring were the slave islands of the Caribbean, whose brutalised inhabitants were in no position to complain.

Dutch dominance of the herring trade had been built on quality control, technical innovation and state protection. When, after centuries of indolence, the penny finally dropped for the British, it was the Scottish fishery in particular that led the way. In the 1750s, a raft of legislation introduced a system of bounties for anyone prepared to build Dutch-style herring busses. Between 1762 and 1796, Scotland doubled the size of its fleet and its catch tripled as a result. Investment by the Highland Society of London, a group of wealthy Scots who supported the building of new fishing villages to employ tenants displaced by the Highland Clearances, added to that momentum. Then, when Scottish curers at last managed to replicate the delicacy and consistency of the Dutch cure (shamelessly rebranded as the 'Scotch cure'), and the 1825 abolition of the swingeing duty on salt made the production of high-quality white herring much cheaper, access to the lucrative markets of northern Europe opened up for the first time. The coming of the railway, which made possible the rapid transportation of fresh or lightly preserved fish, changed the domestic market too and rang the death knell for the little-lamented red herring. The kipper – gutted, split, then gently smoked – was invented in North Shields in the 1840s by John Woodger: surely the absolute apogee of the preserved herring. The Yarmouth bloater, popularised around the same time, was similar in the lightness of the cure, but left whole in the old English manner, giving a slightly richer taste.

Booming at last after centuries of mediocrity, the British fisheries hitched themselves to the propulsive thrust of the industrial revolution and fashioned a fishing operation unprecedented in its scale and sophistication. The introduction of large steam-powered ships reinvigorated the nation's historic ports, and the waters around Great Britain groaned under a vast armada of boats, which were followed from fishery to fishery by an itinerant army of highly skilled Scottish 'fisher lassies', who gutted and salted the catch with breath-taking velocity. In 1913, the UK shipped three and a half billion cured herring overseas, eighty per cent of them to Germany and Russia. Then war broke out with Germany, the Russian revolution burst into flames, and everything fell apart.

By 1934 the British catch was half that of its pre-war peak. The Herring Industry Board, set up by the government to arrest this decline, attempted to persuade the British public to eat more herring, but with little success: like offal, this bony fish was becoming increasingly lumbered with the unattractive aura of 'poor people's food'. ('The barrel always smells of herring,' is an old French taunt towards those whose aspirations outstrip their modest station, and a similar snobbery flourished on these shores too.) The board's next gambit was to open factories that turned herring into food supplements, fishmeal and animal fodder, and by 1950 almost half of the nation's catch was being industrially processed, with catastrophic consequences. Unlike the makers of kippers, bloaters or Scotch-cured white herring, pet food and fish oil manufacturers cared little about the size of the fish or the gentleness with which they were handled, meaning that the fishermen who supplied them could embrace the efficient but damagingly indiscriminate system of pelagic trawling – huge cone-shaped nets towed through the midwater, often behind two boats, cutting through the shoals like a warmed-up ice cream scoop.

In the decades that followed, immature fish were dragged out of the waters in horrific quantities, recruitment levels dropped like a stone, and stocks collapsed. This all happened in plain sight, but the sea fishing sector's tendency towards international arm-wrestling stood in the way of effective remedial measures being adopted. In 1977, with an irreversible apocalypse looming, the British government unilaterally declared a ban on herring fishing in its North Sea waters, leading to a tense but rather nostalgic encounter between Royal Navy ships and Dutch trawlers. Other European nations reluctantly followed suit, implementing bans of their own. While this draconian development did allow stocks to partially recover, it also hammered several nails into the coffin of Britain's centuries-old North Sea fisheries (and led to a similar collapse in the herring population off the west of Scotland after the trawlers relocated there to escape the ban). After the embargo was lifted in 1983, EU quotas and a continent-wide waning in demand allowed the fish to continue their revival.

Herring from fisheries deemed sustainable by the Marine

Stewardship Council are now easy to come by, and trad-itional British producers, particularly in Scotland, continue to make exceptional cured and smoked fish. But this is a fish that, on these islands at least, has been pushed to the margins. You may come across the odd kipper on a hotel breakfast menu, or perhaps a little fillet, lightly soused, as a delicate starter somewhere modern and whitewashed. You may find fresh herring on some fishmongers' counters too. Very little, though, will have been caught by British boats. The herring once decided the destiny of empires; our failure to care for it helped decide the destiny of Britain's fisheries. In ports like Great Yarmouth, Lowestoft, Grimsby and Scarborough – towns that were built on herring bones long before Amsterdam was – fishing has become a largely peripheral pursuit. Whatever happens in the post-Brexit age, it is hard to see it being substantially revived. That ship – quite heartbreakingly – appears to have sailed.

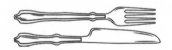

CINNAMON

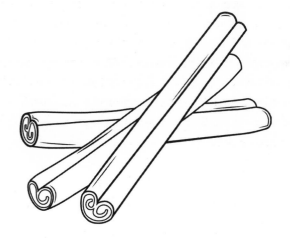

I N A PARTIALLY LOST ROMANTIC poem, known a little unromantically as *Fragment 44*, the Greek lyric poet Sappho told of the spectacular wedding of Andromache, a beautiful, virtuous Cilician princess, and Hector, the doomed heir to the throne of Troy. As the streets of Troy filled with people and 'a wondrous echo reached the heavens,' spices were burned to mark their nuptials: 'Myrrh and cassia and frankincense were mingled. / And the older women wailed aloud. / And all the men gave forth a high-pitched song.'

Sappho, who composed these lines on the island of Lesbos around 600 BCE, clearly thought of the dried bark of the cassia tree – a species of cinnamon – as the kind of luxurious offering that would please the nostrils of these mythical royals. And reading the report of another Hellenic heavyweight, Herodotus, the reason for its rarefied status seems abundantly clear. The Arabs who gathered cassia were forced, the historian wrote, to 'bind ox hides and other skins all over their bodies and faces except for the eyes'. This protective clothing was required because the spice, which grew in a shallow lake, was guarded by 'winged creatures, very like bats, that squeak similarly and make a fierce resistance'. No wonder it didn't come cheap.

Getting hold of cassia was a walk in the park, though, compared with sourcing the closely related spice known simply as cinnamon. This, Herodotus stated, could only be found in a place dominated by giant 'cinnamon birds', which 'take these dry sticks . . . and carry them off to nests stuck with mud to precipitous cliffs, where man has no means of approach'. To get to the prized aromatics, the Arabs 'cut dead oxen and asses and other beasts of burden into the largest possible pieces,' to use as a lure. As the birds greedily hoarded this gory flesh, gravity eventually intervened and their overloaded nests came crashing down, showering the ground with sticks of cinnamon (and bloody chunks of cow). In the fourth century BCE, the philosopher Aristotle lent weight to the cinnamon bird story but intimated that the Arabs had perhaps refined their approach: 'They say that the inhabitants attach leaden weights to the tips of their arrows and therewith bring down the nests, and from the intertexture collect the cinnamon sticks.' But Theophrastus, who succeeded Aristotle as the head of the Athenian Lyceum, had a different theory altogether: as far as he was concerned, cinnamon wasn't hoarded by birds, it was guarded by 'deadly snakes'.

A few centuries later, Pliny the Elder, in *The Natural History* (77–79 CE), would scornfully dismiss all talk of bats, birds and serpents, blaming the prevalence of such tall stories on the Del Boy-like patter of spice sellers. 'All these tales have been evidently invented for the purpose of enhancing the prices of these commodities,' he wrote – a cynical accusation, but one with a loud ring of truth to it.

What is indisputable is that the yarns spun by Greek commentators showed just how ill-equipped they were, despite their vast erudition, to fathom the size of the Asian continent and the true nature of the spice trade that traversed it. Herodotus believed Arabia to be 'most distant to the south of all inhabited countries,' and the sole source of these expensive aromatics, but on both counts he was completely wrong. Cinnamon is obtained from the inner bark of several closely related trees, all of them native to parts of the world considerably more distant than Arabia. And though the Arabs were the middlemen who sold it to the Greeks, they played no part in its harvest. The sweetest, most delicate variety, known as true cinnamon or Ceylon cinnamon, is taken from the *Cinnamomum verum* tree of Sri Lanka and southern India. *Cinnamomum burmannii*, thicker, darker and more robust, hails from Indonesia. The spice we know as cassia, the most aggressively pungent of the family, comes from the *Cinnamomum cassia* tree, which grows in southern China and northern Vietnam.

With their symphonic impact on the senses, impressive durability and often highly localised sources, spices of every kind were among the principal engines of international commerce in the ancient world, but, at a time when most people lived and died in the region of their birth without ever leaving it, the distances involved defied comprehension. The cassia written about by Sappho and Theophrastus had travelled thousands of kilometres from China to Greece, passed from hand to hand by nomadic tribespeople in exchange for food, fabrics, dyes, metals or whatever else happened to be in high demand. Cinnamon had come a similarly long way, either overland through India or on boats across vast stretches of the Indian Ocean and Red Sea to the entrepôt ports of the Middle East. To many

Greeks, the realities of the spice trade – a complex chain of mundane transactions between dozens of disparate people, each of whom was blind to the existence of most of the others – would have seemed far more implausible than the idea of a shallow lake protected by killer bats.

Arab tribesmen, with their slow but durable caravans of single-humped camels, were heavily involved in the trafficking of cassia and cinnamon, but they were far from alone. The Phoenicians, the great seafarers of the ancient Mediterranean, established a maritime trade with India – analysis of the contents of flasks found at various archaeological sites suggests that cinnamon was being brought to the Levant by Phoenician sailors around three thousand years ago – and the Jews, too, were regular buyers of spices from far-flung corners of the world, often for use in olive oil-based perfumes. Cinnamon and cassia were mentioned frequently in the Old Testament – a woman's garments were said to smell of cassia in one of the Psalms, while in Proverbs an adulterous harlot told her lover: 'I have perfumed my bed with myrrh, aloes, and cinnamon. Come, let us take our fill of love until the morning.' Both spices were also included in the recipe handed down from God to Moses to make an 'oil of holy ointment' with which to bless the Tabernacle. In neighbouring Egypt, Asian spices were used to embalm the dead – the Greek historian Diodorus described how Egyptians would 'carefully dress the whole body for over thirty days, first with cedar oil and certain other preparations, and then with myrrh, cinnamon, and such spices as have the faculty not only of preserving it for a long time but also of giving it a fragrant odour'.

The elite of Rome, that most exuberantly global of cities, loved spices as much as they adored an orgy and a good war. Cinnamon and cassia were both used in large quantities in ritual, religion, personal grooming (aromatic unguents being very much in vogue) and, to a lesser extent, food. Pliny saw fit to describe the flavour of the worst cinnamon ('acrid') and the best cassia ('extremely hot to the taste, that it may be said to burn the tongue, rather than gradually warm the mouth') and elsewhere made brief mention of a cinnamon-infused wine, but these aromatic spices were more often used to stimulate the nostrils than the palate – never more extravagantly than when Emperor Nero came to mourn his wife in 65 BCE (having kicked her to death, according to some sources). 'Those who are likely to be the best acquainted with the matter assert that this country does not produce in a whole year so large a quantity of perfumes as was burnt by the Emperor Nero at the funeral obsequies of his wife Poppæa,' wrote Pliny.

Even though the efficiencies brought by the Roman empire made trade between Asia and Europe smoother and faster than ever before, that didn't mean it was necessarily much better understood. Pliny's account of the cinnamon trade managed to be both highly detailed and deeply confusing: the spice, he wrote, was bought by Troglodytae ('cave dwellers') from their neighbours, the Ethiopians, then carried on a five-year round trip 'over vast tracts of sea, upon rafts, which are neither steered by rudder, nor drawn or impelled by oars or sails'. This dangerous journey ended at an Arabian port he called Ocilia – a town in the kingdom of the Gebanites, whose ruler guarded the right to regulate the onward sale of cinnamon, the price of which he kept deliberately and maliciously high. In 'return for their wares' the cave dwellers 'bring back articles of glass and copper, cloths, buckles, bracelets, and necklaces; hence it is that this traffic depends more particularly upon the capricious tastes and inclinations of the female sex'. Many elaborate theories have been constructed about who the cave dwellers and Ethiopians of Pliny's telling might have been, but unlike his contempt for women, which was clearly razor sharp, his geography was frustratingly opaque.

After the disintegration of Rome's western empire, the transport of spices from Asia to Europe reduced to a trickle, but the trade was revived on an even grander scale after the seventh century, as the blossoming of Byzantium and the rapid expansion of Islam laid the foundations for a golden age of commerce between east and west. In the eleventh century, Simeon Seth, the Jewish-Byzantine scholar, was noting that the very best cinnamon could be bought in the Iraqi city of Mosul, suggesting that spice routes from India had been re-established. The most beautiful and revealing of medieval Arab cookbooks, *Kitab al-Tabikh*, written in 1226 by a scribe known as al-Baghdadi, made clear that these spices were readily available and deeply embedded in the region's cuisine – far more so than had been the case in ancient Greece and Rome. Cinnamon, which he said should be 'rough, thick, tightly coiled, with a penetrating aroma, burning to the tongue,' appeared in the vast majority of the book's meat, fish and vegetable dishes, in every conceivable form: whole, pounded, scraped or ground, added early to slow-cooked dishes or else sprinkled at the finish. It was, however, completely absent from the book's sweetened dishes – in thirteenth-century Baghdad, unlike twenty-first century northern Europe, cinnamon was seemingly not a spice for the dessert section.

The main couriers of spices into Europe were Venetian traders, who picked them up from the ports of Byzantium and the Islamic world, most notably Constantinople and Alexandria, then moved them on to markets in Britain, Germany, France and Flanders – it was the profits accrued from their sale that helped turn Venice into the magnificent spectacle we see today. Here, cinnamon's vast expense limited its use to the households of the very rich, in which it was thrown around with carefree abandon. In the royal cookbook *The Forme of Cury* (c.1390), 'powdour of canel' or 'flour of canel' (a word derived from the Latin *cannella*, meaning 'little tube') featured in recipes for everything from swan to rabbit, eel to lamprey. One of the defining sauces of Europe's fanciest kitchens was camelyne, a mix of bread-crumbs, vinegar, sometimes nuts and fruit, and almost always a big hit of cinnamon and ginger.

Like most spices, cinnamon and cassia were considered potent pharmaceuticals as well as flavourings. This belief had its roots in the writings of the classical physicians whose wisdom was adopted and adapted throughout Europe and the Muslim world. The ancient Greek pharmacologist Dioscorides had described cinnamon as 'warming, diuretic, softening and digestive,' with uses that ranged from carrying out abortions to reducing freckles and sunburn, and cassia was presumed to have similar qualities, but with less potency: 'If there is no cinnamon at hand then twice as much [cassia] mixed with medicines will do the same thing.' Clear echoes of this could be detected hundreds of years later and a long way from Greece in the Venerable Bede's commentary *On the Song of Songs*, in which the eighth-century Northumbrian cleric noted the distinction between cassia and cinnamon and explained that the former is 'useful for curing the ailments of many bodily organs,' while the latter is 'twice as efficacious' as a medicine. In Galenic terms, physicians considered these spices to be extremely hot and fairly dry, which meant they worked to counter problems caused by cold and moist humours, including many congestive illnesses common in these northern climes. The twelfth-century German abbess, philosopher and natural historian Hildegard of Bingen stated that cinnamon, heated with good wine, could cure fevers and gout, and that a heavy head and blocked nose would be cleared if the spice were eaten with bread or licked from the hand.

The hotness of character that made cinnamon efficacious against a head cold also gave it another much sought-after benefit. An excess of humoural coldness was thought to result in a lack of sexual interest or capability, so hot spices would be of considerable benefit, even though their dryness might, it was believed, inhibit fertility. In one of the stories of Geoffrey Chaucer's *The Canterbury Tales*, Januarie, an ageing knight, marries a much younger woman called May, who will, inevitably, end up cuckolding him with a squire. To keep his 'courage' strong enough for his fecund bride to be satisfied, Januarie 'drynketh ypocras, clarree, and vernage / Of spices hoote'. Hippocras, to use its more familiar spelling, was a spiced wine widely consumed throughout Europe for the same reasons as the pharmaceuticals peddled today by email spambots. Among its supposedly potent ingredients, cinnamon was the most prominent.

Le Ménagier de Paris (1393), a French treatise on wifely obedience, said of hippocras that, among the many spices used, 'the cinnamon and the sugar should dominate'. John Russell, usher and marshal to Humphrey, Duke of Gloucester, provided two recipes for hippocras in his *Boke of Nurture* (c.1460–70) – a posh one that included cinnamon, grains of paradise and sugar, and one 'for commyn people' based on cheaper ingredients: cassia (which he called 'canelle'), long pepper and honey.

As those email spammers know only too well, there is plenty of money to be made from the promise of chemically enhanced performance, so when Christopher Columbus set off across the Atlantic in 1492 in search of a westward route to Asia, among the treasures he hoped to bring back were those much desired but wildly expensive Asian spices. If he could circumvent the long and complex overland spice routes, along which countless middlemen drove prices ever higher, the promise of a great fortune awaited. Having 'succeeded' in his quest to reach the Indies – actually the Bahamas, Cuba and Hispaniola – Columbus was convinced that he had discovered a gateway to the aromatic riches of the Orient. 'I believe that I have found rhubarb and cinnamon,' he wrote to King Ferdinand of Spain, 'and I shall find a thousand other things of value.' The second part of that statement had some truth to it; the bit about cinnamon didn't. What he had actually found was some Caribbean tree bark.

On Columbus's second voyage, even the expedition's doctor, a man steeped in the knowledge of spices, became a fool to his own wishful thinking. In a letter outlining his experiences, Diego Alvarez Chanca wrote: 'A sort of cinnamon also has been found; but, to tell the truth, it is not so fine as that with which we are already acquainted in Spain. I do not know whether this arises from ignorance of the proper season to gather it, or whether the soil does not produce better.' The problem wasn't the soil or the season; the problem was that the world's entire supply of cinnamon was located thousands of miles away in Asia.

Long after the realisation had sunk in that the Americas were not the Indies, the Europeans' wistful search for New World cinnamon continued unabated. This reached a tragic nadir in 1540, when the conquistador Gonzalo Pizarro drove an expedition of two hundred and fifty Spaniards and four thousand natives into the jungles of Ecuador in search of El País de la Canela – the mythical 'land of cinnamon' – which, through a combination of European delusions and the understandable unwillingness of the South Americans to rile their cruel, trigger-happy visitors, was consistently and confidently predicted to be just a few days' march away. Two years later, after a long descent into starvation, rage and unfettered savagery, Pizarro returned with around eighty surviving companions and absolutely no cinnamon.

While the Spanish were desperately sniffing American bark and hoping it might be cinnamon, their great rivals, the Portuguese, were finding a slow, dangerous but ultimately successful way of muscling in on the sourcing of Asian spices: sailing to India. In May 1498, Vasco da Gama, having circumnavigated the African continent and crossed the Arabian Sea, arrived in Calicut, the great trading port of India's Malabar coast, 'in search of Christians and spices'. As annual armadas followed in da Gama's wake, Portugal's new spice barons became increasingly aware that the best cinnamon in Malabar's magnificent markets hailed not from the Indian mainland but from a nearby island referred to variously as Ceilam, Cillam, Zilon or Zallon: Sri Lanka.

The Portuguese weren't the first outsiders to discover the source of this exceptional spice – the Moroccan scholar and explorer Ibn Battuta, who visited south Asia in the 1330s and 1340s, described seeing a Sri Lankan shoreline 'covered with cinnamon trees brought down by torrents and heaped up like hills on the shore,' and explained how merchants from Malabar, the coastal region at the heart of the Indian spice trade, would sail over to load up in exchange for gifts of 'woven stuffs', which they presented to the tyrannical local sultan – but they were the first to make moves to snatch it all for themselves.

In 1505, Dom Lourenço de Almeida, son of the first viceroy of Portuguese India, landed in Sri Lanka and immediately extracted a hefty tribute, paid in cinnamon, from the King of Kotte, one of several rival kingdoms on this politically fractured island. Returning in force and taking advantage of Sri Lankan divisions, the Portuguese built a fortress at Colombo in 1517 and took control of much of the island's coast – and with it the European cinnamon trade. This domination lasted for just over a century. Then the Dutch, who had generously offered to assist the King of Kandy, the largest Sinhalese kingdom, in seeing off the Portuguese, violently reneged on their treaty, kept the lands for themselves and then, to pile misery upon misery, set about persecuting any Catholic Sri Lankans who had previously been forced to convert by their Iberian overlords. It was the Dutch who built the first commercial cinnamon gardens around Colombo – previously all Sri Lankan cinnamon had grown wild – and turned the cinnamon trade into a highly controlled monopoly. This monopoly would be toppled in 1815 when the British arrived in Sri Lanka with their gunboats and suggested to the Dutch that maybe they should be in charge now, then brutally colonised the kingdom of Kandy for good measure. No longer controlled by colonial powers, Sri Lankan cinnamon is well worth seeking out today, either ground or whole. Gentle, slightly earthy, beautifully aromatic, it's a world away from the ground cinnamon sold in supermarkets, which tends to actually be Chinese cassia – cheap, plentiful and unsubtle in character.

As the availability of cinnamon expanded in step with European control of the trade, its place in the British kitchen underwent a slow but significant evolution. In tandem with sugar – once an exotic flavouring added in small quantities to medieval fish, meat and vegetable dishes, but whose use narrowed as its availability grew and the distinction between sweet and savoury foods became more defined – cinnamon came to be valued more for its inherent sweetness than for its spicy complexity. This change was gradual: *A Book of Cookrye*, published in London is 1591, listed cinnamon as a flavouring for baked pig, mutton balls, sparrow stew and the wonderfully named 'pudding in a turnep root', while also incorporating 'sugar, sinamon and ginger' as a trinity of flavourings in a dozen different fruit tarts, a sweet 'buttered loaf' and a dish of stuffed pears (the instructions for which, rather beautifully, require the cook to fill the fruit with 'sugar, ginger, sinamon, more sinamon, then ginger'). By the time Hannah Glasse was writing *The Art of Cookery Made Plain and Easy* (1747), cinnamon was featuring in a litany of desserts – fruit puddings, rice puddings, cakes, custards, pancakes, chocolate – but was almost entirely absent from the savoury side.

Uses of the spice have broadened out again in recent decades as our appetite for Asian and Levantine flavours has expanded, but it remains predominantly a spice for cakes, buns and just about anything containing both sugar and egg. It's there in mulled wine, too, of course – the modern version of hippocras: no longer widely regarded as a health drink, but potentially still a fuel for passion. Depending on how your Christmas party unfolds.

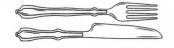

BANANAS

I N 1999, ARCHAEOLOGISTS AT THE site of the new City Hall building in Southwark, a couple of minutes' stroll from Borough Market, announced that a near-complete banana skin had been found preserved within the water-logged environs of a fifteenth-century fish farm, together with several random pieces of antique refuse: carpenters' tools, pewter spoons, a bowling ball, a bottle in a wicker basket. This eye-opening discovery, heralded by the Museum of London, made national headlines ('Britain's first banana found in Tudor rubbish,' trumpeted the *Guardian*) and overturned many preconceptions about the extent of medieval trade. 'Since it was found on a historical site that had not been disturbed before, museum staff are sure [the banana skin] is not simply a piece of modern-day London litter,' the BBC reported. When subsequent analysis made clear that the blackened peel was, without a shadow of a doubt, simply a piece of modern-day London litter, the museum's terse clarification was far less widely reported.

That this story caught the attention of the national media is emblematic of the prominence afforded to a tropical import that has, somehow, become an unlikely cornerstone of the British diet. By volume, the banana – a conveniently self-contained package of calorific ballast so soft and sweet that even the fussiest of children will eat one without complaining – accounts for around a quarter of all fruit eaten in the UK, a remarkable state of affairs for a country perfectly suited to producing a farrago of delicious fruits, all of which categorically aren't bananas. So central has it become to our food culture that when anti-European campaigners sought in recent decades to stoke fears of EU overreach, one of the stories they liked to tell was about the bloc's (entirely imagined) desire to ban curved bananas. In his days as a hucksterish Brussels correspondent, it was bananas and prawn cocktail crisps that future prime minister Boris Johnson chose to construct as the sacred cows most at risk from the malevolent forces of Europe – and if a nation's tastes can be judged by the scare stories that raise its pulse, this tells us something quite profound about the food preferences of modern Britain.

Bland and unremarkable though the banana may now seem, the story of its journey to ubiquity – not just here but in the United States, home of the banana split, banana milkshake and banana pancake – is a dramatic and deeply unedifying one. Or at least the most recent part of it is. The banana has two distinct histories, one for each hemisphere: in the east, a gentle tale of evolution, cultural exchange and glorious biodiversity; in the west, a short, sharp, traumatic explosion, driven by impressive innovation and entrepreneurship but pockmarked by exploitation, corruption and environmental disaster.

It all began in the tropical forests of Asia, where dozens of wild banana species continue to thrive, including two from which all cultivated varieties are derived: *Musa acuminate*, which grows on the Malay Peninsula, Indonesia and Papua New Guinea, and *Musa balbisiana*, which covers a band across eastern India, mainland Southeast Asia and southern China. The banana tree is, to western eyes, compellingly strange. It's not even really a tree, but a massive perennial herb. Its trunk, which emerges from an underground organ known as a rhizome, isn't really a trunk, but a tight spiral of overlapping leaf sheaths. Suspended beneath its canopy of enormous leaves, clamped to a pendulous peduncle (one of the great words of botanic vocabulary), hangs an improbably vast array of fingers – all of which are clearly the wrong way up – and, swaying below them, a massive, triffid-like male flower. After fruiting, which it does just once, this plant dies off, but for several years new pseudo-stems will continue to push up from offshoots on the same rhizome. If an offshoot is carefully removed and planted elsewhere, its base will swell to create a fecund new rhizome of its own, meaning that in the hands of a skilled farmer this horticultural oddity is a gift that keeps on giving.

One of the world's most important archaeological sites is located at Kuk Swamp, a patch of marshy land on Papua New Guinea. Here, in the most watery and backward of backwaters, compelling evidence has been found of the very earliest incidence of *Musa acuminate* domestication, dating to around 5000 BCE. Wild bananas, which reproduce sexually, come packed with shot-like seeds that render them of little culinary use to anyone but the most punctilious of food-preparers, so the trees may initially have been exploited not for their fruit but for the practical use to which their large leaves and strong fibres could be put, or perhaps for the other edible parts: the flower or the starchy rhizome.

Over time, the organised planting of bananas took shape quite independently in other parts of Southeast Asia, leading to the creation of multiple local subspecies. Across several millennia, through migration and trade, these close relatives were carried into each other's habitats, then further north into the realm of *Musa balbisiana*, and the resulting orgy of hybridisation between different species and subspecies led to the emergence of sterile fruits, whose high proportion of sweet pulp, unencumbered by hard seeds, made their propagation more attractive. After millennia of crossing and selection, banana cultivars are now completely barren – those black specks in the middle of their fingers are the dull vestiges of their ancestors' reproductive systems. Today, there are somewhere between five hundred and a thousand cultivars in existence, some of them incredibly localised, ranging in character from small, sweet digits to dense cylinders of starchy flesh that demand to be cooked. We in the west consume but a tiny handful.

As domesticated bananas were disseminated across Asia, they insinuated themselves deep into the cultures of the civilisations that adopted them. In India, bananas appeared in the most ancient of Sanskrit texts, as well as becoming firmly embedded in the subcontinent's cuisine. China, too, readily embraced the genus as it migrated north. In the early third century CE, Yang Fu, an advisor to the Eastern Han court, documented for his northern Chinese masters some of the oddities of his native South China Sea region, including a plant with 'a stem like a bamboo shoot,' the fibres of which were woven into a coarse linen by local women, and 'very sweet' fruit, 'like sugar or honey. Four or five of these fruits are enough for a meal,' he wrote. 'After eating, the flavour lingers on among the teeth.' Around a century later, the Jin Dynasty scholar and botanist Chi Han described the bananas of southern China in more detail: one, 'resembling a sheep's horn in shape,' was 'the sweetest and most delicious in taste;' another, 'resembling a cow's udder,' was slightly inferior; and a third, 'the size of a lotus rootstock,' was not much cop at all.

It was in India, during the campaigns of Alexander the Great, that Europeans first encountered bananas. Theophrastus wrote in his *Enquiry into Plants* (c.350 BCE–c.287 BCE) of one large tree that 'has wonderfully sweet and large fruit; it is used for food by the sages of India who wear no clothes,' and another 'whose leaf is oblong in shape like the feathers of ostrich; this they fasten on to their helmets, and it is about two cubits long'. Either or both of these descriptions could refer to banana trees, as could a similar passage found in Pliny the Elder's *The Natural History* (77–79 CE), which told of a tree whose sizeable leaves resembled 'the wing of a bird' and whose sweet fruit sustained Indian holy men.

Arab and Persian traders, whose continent-spanning exploits were vital to the westward journey of many Indian and East Asian foodstuffs, carried bananas with them to the Levant, and it was from the Arabic *mauz* that the scientific name for the genus, *Musa*, would be adapted. It was also from the Arab lands that bananas were later brought to southern Spain. After the Muslim conquest of the Iberian peninsula in the eighth century, bananas were among the crops introduced to the territories of Al-Andalus.

The Calendar of Córdoba, an Arabic text written in the tenth century that outlined the region's agricultural agenda, described September as the month when 'sugar cane and bananas begin to grow,' and November as the month that 'vegetable seedlings, citron trees, banana trees and jasmines are covered over so that the frost cannot harm them'. Small enclaves of banana production would continue to thrive in southern Spain long after the fall of the caliphate.

Cultivated bananas were carried over the sea from Asia to Africa at some point in the first millennium BCE (the prehistoric trade and migration relationship between the two continents is among the most intriguingly opaque subplots in the history of food) as well as in several subsequent waves, including at least one involving Arab overland trade routes. Africa became a secondary centre of diversification for two major subspecies: one, the East African highland banana, became widely established in the Great Lakes region of East Africa, where it remains a vitally important food (Uganda is regularly among the top ten global producers of bananas, despite having almost no export trade); the other, the African plantain, preserved remains of which were identified in Cameroon dating from between 840 BCE and 350 BCE, became a common staple in the wet, tropical zones of Central and West Africa, where hundreds of distinct local cultivars were developed – a recent study identified ninety-seven in the Democratic Republic of the Congo alone. It was in West Africa, through the Niger-Congo family of languages, that the word 'banana' emerged. And it was also in West Africa that the banana's story took a darker turn.

*   *   *

In the early years of the fifteenth century, the emerging nautical powers of Portugal and Spain set their sights on the Atlantic coast of Africa, hoping to circumvent the land-based onward traffic in the region's valuable natural resources, which had long been controlled by Arabs and Italians. The Portuguese led the way, capturing the busy Moroccan port of Ceuta in 1415, settling the Atlantic islands of Madeira in the 1420s and, in 1434, becoming the first European sailors (or certainly the first to make any noise about it) to find their way around Cape Bojador – a bulging head-land that juts from the western Sahara. In the years that followed, merchants licensed by the Portuguese crown began landing along the Guinea coast, gaining direct access to gold, spices, hardwoods, ivory and slaves. In their wake, Spanish sailors followed, causing no little tension between the Iberian adversaries.

One of the most lucrative of the economic developments sparked by these maritime adventures took place on Madeira, where, in the 1450s, moves were made by the Portuguese to start producing sugar, then still an expensive luxury in Europe. In 1480, in exchange for recognising Portugal's monopoly on trade with 'the islands or lands of Guinea', Spain was granted sole dominion over the Canary Islands, another Atlantic archipelago, and these too were almost immediately seeded with sugar plantations. Producing sugar is a labour-intensive undertaking, and therefore highly expensive – but only if that labour is being paid. Soon, workers from Europe were being supplemented by an ever-increasing number of slaves from the African mainland, and these slaves needed feeding. Thomas Nichols, a merchant from Gloucester who journeyed to the Canary Islands in 1556, wrote of Gran

Canaria's 'singular good wine', its 'twelve sugar houses', and the abundance of a plant he called the 'plantano', the fruit of which was, he wrote, 'like a cucumber, and when it is ripe it is blacke, and in eating more delicate then any conserve'. The Spanish, as well as bringing African slaves to the Canaries, had also introduced African bananas – and they did so not for their own consumption but as an inexpensive staple with which to feed their human chattel.

A pattern was set. When the Spanish landed in the Caribbean at the end of the fifteenth century, their first instinct was to enslave the indigenous people to man their gold mines, but African slaves were soon being shipped out to fill a growing labour deficit caused by overwork and infectious disease. Around the same time, it was becoming increasingly apparent that sugar cane could thrive in the New World – and so too could bananas. Starting in 1516, when the Spanish friar Tomás de Berlanga took several banana plants from the Canaries to the Caribbean island of Hispaniola, wherever sugar and slaves were taken, bananas followed. It was a combination underpinned by a grim logic: the two plants shared similar Southeast Asian roots and thrived in similar conditions, and for the Africans forced to work the plantations, bananas were a familiar and mercifully nutritious foodstuff. The historic connection between the bananas of the Guinea coast and those of the Caribbean was preserved in the region's lexicon – an unripe banana used for cooking is still widely known as a *guineo* – and African cultivars, including the plantain, remain hugely important to West Indian cuisines.

It was from the Caribbean, in the seventeenth century, that Britain received its first fresh bananas, at least one of which was enjoyed by Thomas Johnson, a Yorkshireman who had settled in London and established an apothecary and physic garden on Snow Hill, near Smithfield market. A pioneering field botanist, Johnson spent several years substantially revising John Gerard's *The Herball* – a work, he noted a little cattishly, that showed up its author's 'want of sufficient learning'. Gerard's chapter on the banana justified this swipe. When he compiled his book in 1597, Gerard had only seen a banana in a preserved state, 'brought me from Alepo in pickle,' and his illustration, while matching the description he gave ('like a small cucumber, and of the same bignesse, covered with a thin rinde like that of the fig,') looked very much like the work of a man who was winging it a bit. In 1633, a banana plant was sent to England on a boat from Bermuda to John Argent, president of the College of Physicians of London. Johnson, a friend of Argent's, was among the recipients of the fingers it yielded, as his revisions to *The Herball* recounted: 'The fruit which I received was not ripe, but greene, each of them was about the bignesse of a large beane . . . if you turne the upper side downeward, they somewhat resemble a boat.' After hanging the bananas in his shop until 'the pulp or meat was very soft and tender, and it did eat somewhat like a muske melon,' Johnson added to Gerard's wonky drawing an 'exacter figure of the plantaine fruit' – clearly the work of a man who had been in the same room as a banana.

More than two centuries would pass before bananas began appearing in Britain as anything other than a novelty, and it took the development of the steamship for this to happen. In 1884, the Liverpool-based shipping company Elder Dempster, led by Alfred Jones, established a coaling depot on the Canary Islands, around six days' journey from Britain in these powerful new craft. Jones invested in rebuilding the islands' production of bananas, and Elder Dempster ships on their way back to Liverpool from Africa began picking up consignments of the fruit whenever space allowed.

According to a biography of Jones published in 1914, the banana had previously been 'practically a luxury' in the UK. 'Fruit traders did not consider it of sufficient value to stock to any large extent. It was unknown to the man in the street. Consequently the fruit was expensive, and the imports extremely insignificant in quantity.' On Merseyside, Jones offered subsidies to local costermongers to enable them to sell his bananas at affordable prices – partly out of concern for the diet of the northern poor, partly to help build demand. 'He subsidised retailers on this side to enable the fruit to be sold cheaply, and devoted an enormous amount of time and trouble to popularise the banana,' his biographer explained. 'The results of his efforts are now well known. At the present time the banana is welcomed in the poorest household, as a nourishing fruit within the purchasing power of all. It is as widely distributed to-day as it used to be scarce twenty years ago. This benefit is practically due to the forceful determination of one man alone, for there were many obstacles to overcome and prejudices to be encountered, before the exotic banana came to be added to the list of everyday fruits in this country.'

Jones wasn't entirely alone in his advocacy. In 1887, Edward Wathen Fyffe, a tea importer, took his wife Ida to the Canaries to aid her recovery from tuberculosis and was struck by seeing banana plantations up close. His company,

Fyffes, started bringing the fruit to London in commercial quantities. As steamships ploughed across the ocean loaded with their yellowing haul, Britain became an enthusiastic consumer of bananas and the hub from which the fruit made its way to the rest of Europe. In 1898, the British government, seeking to bolster the economy of Jamaica – a British colony – made a proposal to Elder Dempster, offering to subsidise a fortnightly shipment of Jamaican bananas. Jones at first turned this down – the logistical challenges involved in transporting delicate fruit grown almost five thousand miles away were intimidating – but a doubling of the proposed subsidy and hints of a knighthood did the trick. In 1901, needing more resources to handle the trade, Sir Alfred (those hints were followed up on) merged his business with Fyffes to form Elders & Fyffes. Ever since then, the Caribbean has remained the main source of bananas sold in the UK. Borough Market was for much of the twentieth century an important staging post for this trade – several of the buildings that surround the market (including one still known as The Banana Store) were once banana warehouses.

Over in the USA, a similar surge in demand took place almost exactly in parallel. In 1870, Lorenzo Dow Baker, a gnarly Cape Cod seaman, stopped in Jamaica to repair his ship and decided to load her up with dozens of bunches of bananas, which, in a race against time, he managed to transport to Jersey City quickly enough to sell for a profit. Baker became the USA's first successful banana importer, buying up land in Jamaica to supply his burgeoning venture. In 1885, he partnered with a young Bostonian fruit wholesaler, Andrew Preston, to form Boston Fruit, a company whose pioneering experiments with refrigerated shipping and storage, utilising vast quantities of ice, significantly extended the lifespan and range of its consignments.

In 1876, the banana was still of sufficient novelty to draw crowds to an exhibit at the Centennial Exhibition in Philadelphia, an event that also showcased such cutting-edge inventions as the telephone. By 1905, the journal *Scientific American* was stating: 'Only a few years ago the banana was a luxury in many northern families. Although fairly common on the city markets, it was too expensive to be generally used by most families living in and near the small towns; but now so abundant and cheap as to be a common article of commerce in every corner grocery store, while in the cities it is frequently referred to as the poor man's fruit. There are probably more bananas shipped into the United States than all other tropical fruits combined.'

The only major impediment to the industry's rapid growth was a lack of available land in the Caribbean. This problem was solved in 1900 when Boston Fruit merged with a company owned by Minor Keith, an amoral American entre-preneur who had built a railroad in Costa Rica in exchange for land grants from the Costa Rican government (and at the cost of thousands of his labourers' lives) and planted much of that land with West Indian bananas. Blending Preston's genius for logistics and marketing with Keith's aptitude for building railways and corrupting government officials, the new business, known as United Fruit, gained control of plantations in Ecuador, Colombia, Nicaragua, Guatemala, Panama and Honduras. In the decades that followed, United Fruit – and other smaller competitors built from the same mould – began to exert their influence not only on the diet of the United States but on the politics of Central America. Their relentless hunger for land – the model was to drive the plantations as intensively as possible, then abandon them when yields fell or disease struck – was matched by their appetite for low taxation, cheap labour and pliable governments unwilling to pursue land reform, workers' rights or any share of the profits.

Entire books have been written about the activities of American fruit companies in the 'banana republics' of Latin America – a phrase coined in 1904 by the writer O. Henry – but a few examples will suffice to cast light on their methods:

1. In 1910, Samuel Zemurray, then a small-scale American banana entrepreneur and later president of United Fruit, contracted two soldiers of fortune with names almost too gangsterish to seem credible – Guy 'Machine Gun' Molony and Lee Christmas – to overthrow the government of Honduras and install an exiled politician, Manuel Bonilla, as his company's puppet.

2. Eighteen years later, United Fruit was accused of encouraging the Colombian government to massacre in cold blood more than a thousand plantation workers who were striking over pay and working conditions – an atrocity depicted in the climactic scene of Gabriel García Márquez's *One Hundred Years of Solitude*.

3. In 1954, Jacobo Arbenz, the leftist president of Guatemala, was ousted by a CIA-sponsored coup having two years

earlier issued a decree allowing the government to redistribute to local peasants any large-scale unused farmland – United Fruit, which owned around seventy per cent of the country's agricultural land, three-quarters of which was fallow, was up to its neck in the US government's decision to intervene.

4. As recently as 2007, Chiquita (United Fruit, but with a new name – a change driven in part by its tainted reputation) reached a plea deal with the US Department of Justice in which the company admitted to paying security fees to an extreme right-wing militia group with a major presence in the Colombian drug trade.

Elected governments and striking workers proved far easier to crush than a pathogen known as Panama disease. This deadly blight, which attacks the roots of banana trees, first appeared in Panama in 1903. Its impact was brutal, exacerbated by the fact that just about every commercial plantation in the Americas was, when the disease first hit, reliant upon a single banana variety, which proved highly susceptible. Known originally as the Figue Baudin ('Baudin's fig'), this variety – notable for its hardy, transport-friendly skin – was transplanted from Southeast Asia to the Caribbean island of Martinique in the early nineteenth century by the French botanist whose name it adopted. Within a few decades it had spread to other islands and been renamed Gros Michel ('big Michael') – its fingers were certainly larger than most sweet bananas, but who Michel was, no one has the slightest clue.

As Panama disease began to threaten the existence of the

ubiquitous Gros Michel, the American growers' response was to abandon their blighted lands and wipe out even more ecosystems in the hunt for virgin soil. By the 1950s, United Fruit's great rival Standard Fruit (known today as Dole), whose comparatively meagre access to land made the urgency of finding a sustainable solution more compelling, had alighted upon a fix: the Cavendish banana, smaller and more fragile than the Gros Michel, but – crucially – disease-resistant (or so it seemed). Native to China but named after the English family on whose Chatsworth estate one of its trees had been planted in the 1830s, this soft, delicate cultivar quietly gained in popularity in Asia and Africa throughout the nineteenth century, but had never previously been grown in the Americas in significant quantities. Standard Fruit's decision to plant Cavendish trees while experimenting with new shipping techniques that could mitigate the fruit's less robust nature soon paid dividends and other banana companies quickly followed suit. The last large consignment of Gros Michel bananas landed in 1965. Since then, almost every sweet banana consumed in the west has been a Cavendish.

The industry's next big fight would come in the form of a rumbling trade dispute. In 1913, United Fruit had gained control of the British importer Elders & Fyffes, meaning that for most of the twentieth century, the US giant was able to profit from the European banana trade. Then, in 1986, Fyffes was taken over by an Irish company, and within a few years found itself embroiled in a bitter battle with its former owners over access to bananas from Honduras, with the newly renamed Chiquita accused of illegally destroying its rival's shipments while bribing local judges to validate its actions. This roughhousing between Europe and America spiralled into something much larger when, in 1993, the EU chose to implement a new system of tariffs and quotas designed to counter the competitive advantages enjoyed by the US banana corporations, whose model involves tightly controlling production (and profits) in Latin America, and favour instead the plantations of former European colonies in Africa, the Caribbean and the Pacific, which tend to be locally owned. The American government reacted aggressively, with the Clinton administration making a formal complaint to the World Trade Organization (twenty-four hours later, Chiquita's CEO made an entirely coincidental $500,000 donation to the Democratic Party). This resulted in a full-scale trade war, which was settled in favour of the Americans in 2009, much to the distress of the world's smaller banana producers.

The biggest challenge now facing producers all over the world is the Cavendish's increasing susceptibility to pathogens, including both Panama disease (it wasn't so resistant after all) and black Sigatoka fungus. Challenges remain for ethically minded consumers, too, with banana-eating still something of a moral minefield. Vitally, Fairtrade bananas are now widely available in the UK, making up around a third of all purchases. It has also been a while since a banana company was directly implicated in a massacre or a coup, but scandals around the widespread use of child labour and poverty wages, the suppression of unions (and violent deaths of labour organisers), and the continued use of dangerous pesticides still bubble away – there are numerous court cases still in progress around the world relating to the employment by major banana companies of a chemical known as DBCP, which destroyed the sperm counts of workers.

The story of the banana has come a long way: from the fruits being rendered sterile for the benefit of eaters to peasants being rendered sterile for the benefit of neo-colonialist corporations. It is up to us to ensure that the next few chapters are perhaps a little less dark.

PASTA

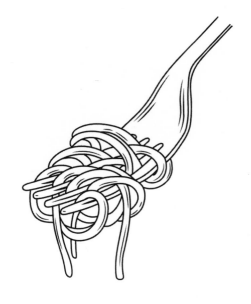

EVERYONE KNOWS THE STORY OF pasta: in the thirteenth century, the Venetian explorer Marco Polo went
to China; there he was fed a big bowl of delicious noodles,
which so thoroughly blew his mind that on his return to
Italy he announced to his fellow countrymen that he'd seen
the future – and it was silky, slick and swimming in sauce.
And just like that, a new culinary universe exploded into
being.

Like a hearty serving of freshly cooked gnocchi, this
story is, of course, a pile of steaming balls. When Marco
Polo set off for the east his homeland was already flush
with pasta. The myth of his role isn't even a particularly
old one, having first appeared in an article in the October
1929 edition of an American trade magazine, *The Macaroni
Journal*, which set out how one of Polo's crewmen, whose
name was Spaghetti, was, through 'signs and gestures',
taught the way of pasta by a Chinese woman. 'Upon
Spaghetti's arrival home, the popularity of this new delicacy soon spread among the villagers, and before long a
similar food made of home grown wheat was to be found
on every table.' In reality, the word 'spaghetti' is derived
from the Italian for 'little strings', and *The Macaroni*

Journal's anonymous writer was either extremely stupid or not entirely serious.

Yet for all its obvious silliness, this story does contain just the tiniest kernel of something true. Pasta – an energy-rich food made by kneading, shaping and boiling wheat flour dough – is inextricably associated with Italy, and with very good reason, but some other parts of the world, including China, developed their own native forms of pasta long before spaghetti became a regular part of the Italian diet.

Known generically as *bing* – a word that covered many wheaten products, including bread – wheat noodles were well established in China by the turn of the third century CE, when varieties such as 'broth bing', 'string-shaped bing' and 'foreign bing' were included in *Shiming*, a dictionary of the Eastern Han dialect. Around a hundred years later, Shu Xi, one of the great scholars of the Western Jin era, wrote *Ode to Bing*, a beautiful paean to pasta. His description of shapes such as 'dog tongues', 'piglet ears' and 'dagger laces' foreshadowed the poetry of the Italian pasta names that would emerge many centuries later – linguine ('little tongues'); orecchiette ('little ears'); vermicelli ('worms') – and his portrayal of the preparation of parcels of dough, 'soft as silk floss in the springtime,' filled with pork rib or mutton shoulder, was deeply sensual: 'The steam billows out into a swelling cloud. / The aroma flies into the air and flees into the distance, / Trailing away, making the loiterer's mouth water.'

While the ancient Chinese salivated over these delicate ravioli-like delights, Europe remained strangely blinkered to the breadth of possibilities contained within an ear of

wheat, instead sticking limpet-like to the two basic preparations that had sustained the continent since the advent
of agriculture: milling the wheat, kneading the flour into
dough, then baking it into loaves; or else, throwing rougher,
less-processed grains into boiling liquid to create mushes
or gruels. Pasta is a simple and fairly obvious amalgamation
of these two methods – the wheat prepared in the manner
of bread dough, but then either cooked straight away in a
boiling liquid or else dried before it has the chance to prove.
Yet despite Europe's obsession with the cultivation of wheat,
the concept of boiling up small pieces of dough failed to
coalesce to any significant degree, a reflection perhaps of
the overwhelming religious and cultural significance of
bread.

That's not to say, though, that the seeds of Italian pasta's
later emergence weren't sown a long time ago. In Greece,
a form of rolled-out dough known as *itria* is referred to in
several ancient texts (although how it was cooked is not
clear), and the Romans used wheat flour to make *laganum*,
which shared some of the qualities of pasta but was seemingly baked or fried rather than boiled. In the first century
BCE, the poet Horace wrote of enjoying laganum with leeks
and chickpeas after a hard day spent wandering through
the Roman Forum. Around two hundred years later, the
De Re Coquinaria cookbook included a recipe for 'patina
cotidiana' ('an everyday dish'), in which minced sow's udder,
fish and chicken were mixed into a ragù with eggs, seasonings, broth and wine, then poured between layers of
laganum. This was preceded by a very similar dish – but
not so everyday on account of the fancy ingredients – which
swapped sow's udder for belly (with nipples still attached)

and added in the breasts of figpeckers or thrushes. Any of these dishes could, depending on the nature of the dough and the moistness of the sauce, have been something not unlike a lasagne al forno – but equally, they could have essentially been meat pies.

It seems highly likely that this Greco-Latin approach to cooking with wheaten dough lived on in Italy in one form or another without troubling the written record – after the collapse of the Roman empire, as wave after wave of northern European barbarians settled in the holy city with their uncouth appetite for rye bread and pig fat, there wasn't much of a written record to trouble, and certainly not one that bothered itself with what the townspeople and peasants of the peninsula were cooking. On the eastern side of the Mediterranean, though, where the cultural influence of the Greek and Roman empires continued to flourish, we can see quite clearly the development of foods that had their roots in itria and laganum and were unambiguously pasta-like in their conception.

The Jerusalem Talmud, a compilation of Jewish law and theology collated in Israel between the third and fifth centuries CE, contained a detailed discourse on the *hallah* – the portion of dough that Jews were expected to give to the priests as an offering every time they baked bread. Any dough cooked in an oven was clearly subject to the hallah, but according to the Gemara, the section of the Talmud that contains rabbinical discussions relating to specific points of law, a question was raised by a woman as to whether, when she made dough to make 'itrium', which was seemingly exempt from the hallah, but then used a little of the leftover dough to make bread, the latter would be subject to tithing. The implication was obvious: itrium, a word clearly taken from the Greek *itria*, was wheat dough that was cooked in a pan rather than baked in an oven. In essence, pasta.

The ninth- to tenth-century Syriac-Arabic dictionary compiled by the Syrian physician and lexicographer Isho Bar Ali described a string-like dough known as 'itriyya', and later medieval Arab cookbooks commonly used the word to characterise a type of long pasta that was added to soups. The thirteenth-century *Kitab al-Tabikh*, compiled in Baghdad, included a recipe that involved meat, onions, chickpeas, chard and rice being stewed in a spicy broth, with itriyya noodles added at the end. A similar recipe from the same book called for noodles known as 'rashta', described as 'dough kneaded hard and rolled out thin, then cut into fine thongs four finger-widths long'. Other words emerged in the Middle East to describe similar uses of dough, including the Persian *laksha* (first mentioned in a tenth-century recipe for 'wild ass soup' with 'pieces of dough' in it). The linguistic similarity between Persian laksha and 'laksa', the spicy noodle soup of Southeast Asia, is almost certainly not coincidental given the depth of the trading relationship between the two regions.

In 827, North African Arabs landed in Sicily and set about establishing a Muslim emirate that would last for more than two centuries. It was here in Sicily, an island that had for centuries been producing some of the world's best durum wheat (Pliny ranked it second among 'foreign' wheats), that pasta started to evolve into something distinctly Italian. The durum species, which evolved through the selection of a mutant strain of ancient emmer wheat, takes its name from the Latin for 'hard', a reference to the considerable resistance offered during milling by its dark, protein-packed kernels. Known as semolina, the coarse yellow middlings of its grain provide the basis for several Levantine staples, including couscous, bulgur wheat and freekeh. When semolina is ground into flour and moistened with water, the stiff, glutinous dough that results is easy to shape and quick to dry. The special qualities of Sicily's durum wheat, paired with sea breezes and warm sunshine, were ripe for exploitation by the island's Arab and Greco-Latin populations, both of which traditionally knew their way around a ball of dough. This unique blend of environmental and cultural conditions led to the emergence of a new dried form of itriyya – a preserved (and therefore eminently tradeable) product that could be made in large quantities and shipped around the Mediterranean.

Even after the Arab rulers of Sicily were unseated by the Normans in 1130, the island retained its rich multiculturalism. The great Arab geographer Muhammed al-Idrisi made his home in Palermo at the cosmopolitan court of the Norman King Roger II and in 1154 became the first man to write about his adopted homeland's novel commodity, and by extension the first to make an explicit reference to Italian pasta: 'To the west of Termini [close to Palermo] there is a town called Trabia, an enchanting place to live, abounding in streams that drive numerous mills. Trabia sits in a vast plain with many great estates, where great quantities of itriyya are made and exported everywhere, especially to Calabria [a region of southern Italy] and other Muslim and Christian lands; many shiploads are sent.'

The principal exporters of this dried Sicilian pasta were merchants from Genoa, one of medieval Europe's preeminent maritime and financial powers, who provided the main link between the farmers of southern Italy and the increasingly powerful city-states of the north, which needed feeding. Before Idrisi, there were no references in Italian sources to anything that can be clearly identified as pasta. In the centuries that followed, as Genoese traders carried pasta from Sicily – and, increasingly, from Sardinia and the southern parts of the mainland, where durum wheat was plentiful – a trickle of references (beginning with a will from 1279 in which the legacy passed on by Genoese military officer Ponzio Bastone included a barrel of 'macharoni') gradually became a flood, replete with an ever-expanding vocabulary: 'tria', tied to the Greek 'itria' and Arabic 'itriyya'; 'fidei' and 'fidelini', which either evolved from or inspired the Arabic 'fidawsh'; 'vermicelli', meaning 'worms' – a word sufficiently commonplace in the twelfth century that French and German Jews were referring to 'vermishelsh' and 'vrimzlish' respectively in a rehashing of that age-old hallah debate; 'lasagne', which described any kind of flat pasta; 'gnocci', meaning 'knots', a name given to spherical pasta that long pre-dated the use of potato in its construction; 'maccheroni', which throughout Italy was used to describe dried pasta, and in the south was a straightforward synonym for pasta of any type (the use of the word 'macaroni' to specifically describe small pasta tubes is a fairly recent North American development).

It was also Genoese sailors who, through their close commercial ties with Catalonia, took dried pasta to Spain, causing another cultural cross – in Andalusia, which remained at least partially under Muslim control until 1492, various culinary writings contained references to dried pasta before similar Italian sources started mentioning it, even though the pasta itself had been brought from Christian Sicily by Italian traders. For centuries, most of the pasta eaten on the Iberian Peninsula would continue to be imported – a reflection of the superior quality of Italian wheat and the enduring trade and dynastic ties between Spain and southern Italy – but the two culinary cultures would slowly diverge: whereas in Italy the defining method of pasta preparation is to boil, drain and dress it, Spaniards are still more inclined to use it as the Arabs traditionally had: added late to one-pot dishes, to cook in their juices.

The dried pasta of the south sparked a revolution in Italian food, but throughout the rest of the country, where a lack of durum wheat and suitable climatic conditions made the production of a preserved product impossible, most households sated at least some of their growing appetite for pasta with the fresh version, made from common wheat. While too soft to dry fully, wheat flour can still be kneaded into a beautifully elastic dough, perfect for cutting into ribbons or parcels. This is particularly true after the addition of eggs, the proteins of which create the appealing bite the pasta would otherwise lack. In medieval Italy, fresh pasta was made at home by domestic cooks or else produced as a sideline by bakers whose primary employment was in the baking of bread, still the dominant staple.

The production of dried pasta, meanwhile, became increasingly professionalised. In 1571, the Vermicelli Makers' Guild of Naples had its charter approved, and in

1598 the Neapolitan authorities made it a crime, punishable by imprisonment, for anyone to sell pasta who wasn't a member. In 1574, Genoa, which had evolved from being a transporter of pasta to being a notable producer, founded a Fidelari Makers' Guild to support the city's dried pasta industry. That these two cities were the first to offer official recognition – and significant commercial advantages – to their producers was telling. For centuries, Naples and Genoa – or, more broadly, the Ligurian coastline close to Genoa – would remain the twin heartlands of dried pasta production, one at either end of the peninsula's long western coastline. Both boasted warm, breezy climates that made the tricky task of drying their pasta at least vaguely reliable, while Naples had the advantage of being home to some very fine durum wheat: the 'saragolla' variety.

Other pasta-making guilds sprang up throughout Italy in the decades that followed, with professional organisation evolving in step with increased mechanisation. Until the sixteenth century, the craft had been very much a manual one, with the available tools limited to rolling pins, drying racks, simple cutting tools and – most importantly – skilled hands and well-worked arm muscles. The *ferro da maccheroni* ('macaroni iron') was an implement in fairly widespread use – a metal roller with perpendicular grooves, the sharp edges of which would cut strips of pasta from a sheet of dough. In the sixteenth century, a machine known as the *ingegno per li maccheroni* ('macaroni engine') began to appear in the workshops of pasta makers. These extrusion presses forced the dough through a die plate to create evenly shaped pasta, with different plates used to create different shapes and sizes. When the Naples Guild revised its charter in 1579, it stated that 'each shop must absolutely possess its own extrusion press suited to perform the work in question' – a move that clearly distinguished the professionals from the domestic dabblers. Mechanical brakes, used to accelerate the slow and arduous process of kneading dough, also became a common feature of these commercial manufactories.

As manufacturing became easier, pasta's place in the Italian diet became ever more substantial. The well-travelled French clergyman and writer Jean-Baptiste Labat, who lived in Italy for several years at the start of the eighteenth century, was struck by its pervasiveness: 'The amount of pasta that is consumed is surprising; those who have not yet abandoned the old way of living would sooner give up bread than maccheroni or some other kind of pasta. It is the daily soup.' This was particularly true in Naples, whose citizens were mocked by other Italians as *mangiamaccheroni* ('macaroni eaters'). Here, at times when wheat prices were low, pasta became accessible even to the very poor – *I Maccaronari*, a painting by the seventeenth-century artist Micco Spadaro, shows a huddle of rag-swaddled beggars hungrily pawing at a large bowl of pasta ribbons on a dirty, rubble-strewn Neapolitan street. Various eighteenth and nineteenth-century accounts paint a vivid picture of Naples as a town heaving with wooden booths at which locals would eat pasta with their hands (a special skill requiring considerable dexterity). No less a travel writer than the German literary giant Johann Wolfgang von Goethe, who visited Naples in the 1780s, reported: 'The macaroni, the dough of which is made from a very fine flour, kneaded into various shapes and then boiled, can be bought everywhere and in all the shops for very little money. As a rule, it is simply cooked in water and seasoned with grated cheese.'

This tasty combination was far from novel. Indeed, the ties that bind pasta to cheese have been tight since the very start – as early as the 1280s, the wandering monk and chronicler Salimbene di Adam was making reference to a fellow friar's greedy consumption of 'lasagne with cheese' – and the intimacy of their relationship is vividly illustrated in Boccaccio's *Decameron*. Completed around 1353, this masterpiece of Italian prose included a satirical tale about a Basque district called Bengodi, in which could be found 'a mountain all of grated parmesan cheese, whereon abode folk who did nothing but make macaroni and ravioli and cook them in capon broth, after which they threw them down thence and whoso got most thereof had most'. Even in recipe books written by chefs serving the wealthiest of households, cheese was by far the most common pairing for pasta, although spices and – unconscionably to the modern reader – sugar were also scattered with gay abandon over the macaroni of the rich.

Italy's most venerable cookbooks frequently cited geography to describe different styles of pasta, suggesting that the strong regional identities that underpin today's baffling diversity of names, shapes and fiercely expressed rules about saucing have long roots. For example, the fifteenth-century recipe book of Maestro Martino of Como, whose culinary skills were employed by the powerbrokers of the Vatican, included 'maccaroni Siciliani', which used a length of stiff wire to create tubes of pasta, and 'maccaroni Romaneschi' – curled ribbons, not unlike tagliatelle – while Cristoforo di Messisbugo, who served the Duke of Ferrara, would the following century describe 'maccheroni alla Napoletana' as thin strips, cut from a sheet.

The presence of such recipes in fancy cookbooks suggested that pasta was a suitable food for the great and good, despite its simple, quotidian nature. Or at least, fresh pasta, made with eggs for the luxurious touch they brought, was acceptable – the dearth of any mention of dried pasta in these tomes was indicative of a gulf in status between the two forms that remains somewhat in evidence today. According to the early seventeenth-century Piedmontese grocer and writer Guglielmino Prato, commercial makers of dried pasta simply could not be trusted: 'It is customary to purchase fidelini made by pasta makers, with the considerable risk of finding that they have been made with very low quality materials or made with old or spoilt flours, especially during famines, and that is why sensible gentlemen will have the fidelini made by their servants.'

The now near-universal association between pasta and tomato-based sauces is nowhere to be found in these foundational texts of Italian gastronomy. It was in the Kingdom of Naples that the culinary potential of the tomato, a sixteenth-century arrival from the New World, was most enthusiastically embraced, and given the region's historic attachment to pasta, it is highly plausible that it was here that the two were first married in a bowl. But – doubtless to the annoyance of all proud Neapolitans – the first explicit reference to pairing pasta with tomato sauce was recorded in the 1807 volume of *L'Almanach des Gourmands*, a vast repository of culinary wisdom compiled by a Frenchman, Grimod de La Reynière: 'It is possible to mix purees and cheese with vermicelli, and sometimes, in autumn, one can replace them successfully with tomatoes.' It was certainly in Naples, however, that *pasta al pomodoro* was popularised in the nineteenth century. By 1863, when two Neapolitan doctors, Achille Spatuzzi and Luigi Somma, wrote at some length about the diet of the city's proletariat, tomatoes formed 'the customary seasoning for macaroni'.

Dried pasta from Naples and Genoa first arrived in London in the seventeenth century. Perhaps surprisingly, though, the earliest English pasta recipes were set down many centuries earlier, in the court of Richard II. *The Forme of Cury* (c.1390) contained an entry for 'loseyns', whose name and construction had much in common with lasagne: 'Take good broth and do in an earthenpot, take flour of paindemain [a type of bread] and make thereof paste with water and make thereof thin foils as paper with a roller, dry it hard and seethe it in broth, take grated cheese and lay it in dishes with powder douce [a medieval spice mix] and lay thereon "loseyns" boiled as whole as you might and above powder and cheese and so twice or thrice and serve it forth.' A second recipe from the same collection, entitled 'makerouns' (a word clearly inspired by 'maccheroni') outlined a similar process, but with the dough cut 'in pieces' and covered with butter and cheese.

While it remained very much a marginal foodstuff until quite recently (in 1957, an April Fools' Day hoax report on the BBC's *Panorama* programme, which showed a family in southern Switzerland gathering a bumper harvest from their 'spaghetti trees', duped millions of credulous watchers), imported Italian pasta began its slow penetration of Britain's mainstream culinary culture in the nineteenth century. Eliza

Acton's *Modern Cookery for Private Families*, published in 1845 and one of the first cookbooks aimed at the domestic kitchen, made clear that dried pasta of various shapes was widely available, at least in the capital – she wrote that Mr Cobbett's on Pall Mall sold 'all the Italian pastes extremely good,' but that high-quality macaroni could be procured from 'many other houses in London'.

Acton suggested that Naples macaroni, which she characterised as 'large, and somewhat thin,' be boiled for 45 minutes and Genoa macaroni – 'less in size, but more substantial' – for 'nearly or quite one hour,' which even allowing for historical differences in the manufacturing process does suggest the English were not fully on-board yet with the concept of 'al dente' (although, in fairness, the consensus that pasta shouldn't be boiled to within an inch of its life had only recently started to form in Italy, with Naples once again taking the lead). She did, however, decry how some of the nation's cooks would soak dried pasta 'in milk and water for an hour or more, before it is boiled, that the pipes may be swollen to the utmost,' suggesting that this would 'render it pulpy'. Her book contained recipes for pasta-based soups, a Neapolitan beef and tomato 'ragout' (which she clearly didn't trust, as she attributed it to a 'friend' and put its name in quote marks, unlike those of her own recipes), and an unctuous, creamy version of macaroni cheese, topped with breadcrumbs. Her most fantastically British suggestion, though, was for 'curried macaroni': six ounces of cooked pasta dropped into a pint and a quarter of stock or gravy, flavoured with a tablespoon of curry powder – in essence, a curry-flavoured Pot Noodle.

The UK has continued to play fast and loose with a food

that in Italy was becoming ever more tightly defined by the strictures that flowed from both culinary refinement and a strong sense of regional identity. For many twentieth-century Brits, their first and often only experience of pasta came from tins of sweet sauce-swaddled hoops, worms or – mamma mia! – letter shapes, and even as the growth of large supermarkets began to make dried Italian pasta widely available in the 1970s and 1980s, the dishes created in British kitchens tended to be bastardisations at best. As any citizen of Bologna will never tire of telling you, spaghetti bolognese – a dish so embedded in British life that it's the first thing many adolescents learn to cook for themselves – is an entirely alien construct, as representative of the city's cuisine as chicken tikka masala is of the Mughal court.

Back in Italy, industrialisation had a huge impact on the production and consumption of dried pasta. In the nineteenth and twentieth centuries, the historic duopoly of Naples and Genoa was gradually undermined by the development of industrial drying methods, which destroyed the natural advantages offered by the two cities' climates and allowed large-scale pasta factories to flourish in Milan, Florence, Parma and the Tuscan town of Sansepolcro. The invention of ever more powerful machines for kneading and shaping dough proved similarly terminal to the guilds of skilled artisans who had controlled its production for centuries. Pasta became much cheaper as a result, making it accessible for the first time to even the very poorest of rural Italians, many of whose forefathers had lived on little more than roots and leaves.

Since the unification of Italy in the late nineteenth century, food had acted as a powerful accelerant in the forging of a coherent Italian identity, and the increasing universality of pasta helped make it a major source of national and regional pride. It remains Italy in microcosm: the localised specificity of shapes and saucing reflect the country's historic and often deeply fractious hodgepodge of city-states and regional kingdoms, while its presence on the menu everywhere from the islands of the Mediterranean to the mountainous frontier of the north is one of the vital pieces of adhesive that bind the nation together. In the thirteenth century, the Umbrian poet Jacopone da Todi had written: 'He who looks at magnitude is often deceived; a peppercorn beats lasagne for virtue.' Now, in the eyes of most Italians, the virtue of pasta doesn't just win out over pepper. Alongside God, family and football, it outstrips pretty much everything else.

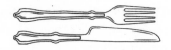

TURKEY

I T IS EMBLEMATIC OF HOW in the world of food the extraordinary can soon become ordinary that the two defining components of the 'traditional' British Christmas dinner – turkey and potatoes – are, at root, as British as the spider monkey and the agave cactus. Like the now deeply humble spud, turkey is a foodstuff that in the modern age has somehow become a byword for blandness. But, like the potato, it was just a few centuries ago a food of great novelty, imbued with all the exoticism of the far-off Americas. Until the start of the sixteenth century, when Spanish invaders made their first wide-eyed incursions into the New World, no European had ever seen a turkey – an extravagantly plumed bird with a placid temperament and the body of a steroid-pumped chicken. Now, it's a much-derided fixture of the supermarket freezer section.

The turkeys we eat today are the tame descendants of the wild turkey, one of two edible fowl domesticated in the Americas. The other, the muscovy duck (which has as much to do with Muscovites as the turkey has with Turks) was an important food source in various parts of South and Central America, but it proved to be far less compelling in its global appeal than the turkey, being neither notably placid nor seemingly steroidal. The wild turkey, a large, non-migratory bird, made its home across almost the entirety of North America, from Ontario in Canada to Veracruz in Mexico, and was, unsurprisingly, a popular source of food for many of the continent's indigenous people. A closely related species, the ocellated turkey – which still lives wild in parts of Belize, Guatemala and Mexico's Yucatán Peninsula – was also eaten, but never domesticated. While it is quite possible to tame an ocellated turkey, when kept in captivity it will reproduce with all the speed and enthusiasm of a particularly world-weary panda.

There were no such problems with wild turkeys: inquisitive, sociable and bold. While they can fly, they're not among nature's most enthusiastic aviators, tending to reserve that ungainly, barrelling but remarkably rapid take-off for times of great menace – and they don't feel menaced by much. The indigenous people of North America had been happily feasting on vast quantities of wild turkey for many centuries, and the same characteristics that made hunting these incautious birds so straightforward also promoted their candidacy for domestication. It was less a case of painstakingly breaking them in, more one of inviting them to stay for the weekend.

Such was the volume of wild turkeys being consumed throughout the continent, and so similar are their bones to those of the domesticated bird, it is hard to pinpoint the timing and location of this shift, but there is evidence that domesticated turkey stocks were established by at least 180 CE within Mexico's Tehuacán Valley. Recent DNA analysis shows that an entirely separate domestication, based on a different subspecies of wild turkey, took place around the same time in the south-west United States.

When the Aztecs settled in the Valley of Mexico and began to build an empire (probably around 1200), turkey husbandry was long established in the region, but it was they who transformed it into an industry. And it was here, in the land of the Aztecs, that Europeans first began to understand its appeal. There is a possibility that the very first European to eat turkey meat was Christopher Columbus, who on 14 August 1502, at the culmination of his fourth voyage to the New World, landed at Punta de Caxinas on the coast of Honduras, where the locals treated him to a feast that included '*gallinas de la tierra*' ('land hens'), a formulation commonly used by Spanish chroniclers to describe the turkey. This was, however, a formulation commonly used by Spanish chroniclers to describe just about every large bird they encountered, such was the inadequacy of the vocabulary at their disposal when confronted by the baffling fauna of an unfamiliar continent, so we can't be entirely sure.

After Hernán Cortés had led his Spanish conquistadores in the swift and brutal subjugation of the Aztec empire between 1519 and 1521, Europeans came into close contact with a society completely in thrall to the turkey. Some of the most colourful early descriptions of the turkey can be found in the writings of the Spanish friar Bernardino de Sahagún. In his *General History of the Things of New Spain*, he wrote of the domesticated turkey that 'it leads the meats; it is the master,' and his breathless enthusiasm bordered on the erotic: 'Tasty, healthful, fat, full of fat, fleshy, fleshy-breasted, heavy-fleshed.' We know from Sahagún that Mexican turkeys were remarkably diverse: 'Some quite black, some like crow feathers, glistening, some white, some ashen, ash coloured, some tawny, some smoky.'

It is also thanks to him that we know of their use in a casserole that few modern cooks would be tempted to reproduce, described in a passage about a wealthy merchant preparing a massive feast for a rather upsetting celebration known as 'the bathing', at which slaves were ceremonially washed and then summarily slaughtered. 'He provided turkeys, perhaps eighty or a hundred of them,' wrote Sahagún. 'Then he bought dogs to provide the people as food, twenty perhaps, or forty . . . at the bottom of the sauce dish they placed the dog meat, on top they placed the turkey as required.'

The one part of the turkey the Aztecs didn't willingly eat was its wattle – the soft, fleshy protuberance that hangs from the bottom of the bird's neck. Instead, they secretly fed it to their enemies, hidden in drinking chocolate: 'One who hates another feeds it to him in chocolate, in sauce; he causes him to swallow it. It is said that he thereby makes him impotent.'

While studiously avoiding the wattle, Aztecs ate turkey in vast quantities – or certainly, rich Aztecs did. Netzahualcoyotzin, the fifteenth-century lord of Texcoco, apparently required a daily tribute of one hundred turkeys. Every person in the town of Mixquiahuala had to contribute to the Emperor Montezuma one turkey every twenty days – a tax that if replicated elsewhere in the region would have generated a mind-bending quantity of birds for the ruler's table. They were certainly needed: the birds of prey in Montezuma's legendary menagerie supposedly munched their way through five hundred turkeys every day, and the people at his court enjoyed similarly unconstrained feasting habits.

For Europeans, whose experience of farmed fowl had hitherto extended little further than chickens (tasty but small) and peacocks (big, beautiful, but frankly horrible to eat), the experience of such feasting had an immediate impact. While many of the new vegetables they encountered in the Americas, such as tomatoes, potatoes and chillies, were initially treated with deep suspicion in the Old World, the turkey was embraced without reservation. The health implications of plants were much worried about, but meat was meat, and Europe had found a capacious and delicious new source.

In 1520, the bishop of Hispaniola sent two turkeys to Lorenzo Pucci, a cardinal in Rome. Around the same time, a few of these giant birds were also seemingly being raised in Spain – and it was in Spain and Italy, then bound together by the ruling Hapsburg monarchy, that this New World arriviste first found favour. Quite when the turkey first made it to England is unclear, but probably the mid-1530s. In 1550, William Strickland, who sailed to the Americas with the Venetian explorer Sebastian Cabot, was granted a coat of arms including 'a turkey-cock in his pride proper,' apparently in celebration of his role in introducing the bird to these shores, but supporting evidence is lacking.

Many thousands of words have been expended on elaborate theories as to how the turkey got its English name – a knotty subject not helped by the fact that other edible birds, including the guinea fowl, were already being described as 'turkey cocks'. By far the most likely explanation is that 'Turkey' or 'Turkish' was used as a shorthand for foreign glamour – maize, also from the Americas, was sometimes referred to as Turkish corn – in the same way that the adjective 'French' was commonly applied by the English to anything a bit unsavoury or venereal. Confusion thus abounded. The lexicographer Samuel Johnson, in the 1755 edition of his dictionary, listed turkey as 'a large domestick fowl brought from Turkey'. In the 1785 edition, he had updated this to say that it was 'supposed to be' brought from Turkey – a clear hedging of bets.

Other nations' linguistic sat-navs proved similarly unreliable. The French went with *coq d'Inde* ('Indian cock') – now shortened to *dinde* – and the Italians initially went for the etymologically similar *gallo d'India*, both of which names also pre-date the arrival of the turkey and were used to describe other exotic birds. The Germans plumped for the highly specific *Calecutische hahn* ('hen of Calcutta'), while the Spaniards kept things simple (for everyone except later historians) by rigidly sticking with the words *gallina* ('hen') and *pavo* – the existing Spanish name for a peacock, a bird whose place on the menu the turkey was destined to steal. The Turks, clearly realising that 'turkey' would be a terrible loan word, went with *hinde*, while the Persians, who were seemingly introduced to the turkey by Armenian traders, deserve praise for choosing the more imaginative 'elephant bird'.

Admired for its impressive scale and exotic aura, the turkey became the centrepiece for some of Europe's most opulent feasts – in 1549, Catherine de Medici had seventy of the birds served to her guests at a Paris banquet – for which it proved an excellent alternative to the once ubiquitous peacock. The turkey may not have been blessed with quite such dramatic plumage (a peacock would usually be served with its head and feathers stitched back on to provide a touch of table-top theatre), but it more than made up for that by actually tasting nice. According to the Spanish writer Gonzalo Fernández de Oviedo y Valdés, its flesh was 'incomparably better and more tender than that of the peafowls in Spain'. Pope Pius V's chef Bartolomeo Scappi agreed, declaring turkey meat to be 'much whiter and softer than that of the common peacock'. His typically appealing suggestion (Pius was a well-fed pontiff) was to blanch the bird in water, lard it with pork fat, stud it with cloves and then spit-roast it slowly.

There was, though, such a thing as too much turkey. In 1541, Archbishop of Canterbury Thomas Cranmer issued an injunction designed to clamp down on the perceived gluttony of English ecclesiasts. In a foreshadowing of George Osborne's insistence that austerity definitely meant being 'in it together', Cranmer selflessly limited his own meal allowance, and that of other archbishops, to a meagre six meat courses and four sweets. The turkey was included in a clause limiting the number of 'greater fishes or fowles' that could be served up: 'There should be but one in a dish, as crane, swan, turkeycock, haddock, pike, tench.' Any greedy ecclesiast wishing to dine on a duo of turkeys with a side of swan would, like it or not, simply have to pull in his belt.

A Book of Cookrye, published in 1584, included the oldest surviving English recipe for turkey – split in two to ensure even cooking, filled with a 'good store of butter,' then baked for five hours – while Thomas Dawson proved in 1587 that no beast is too big for an Englishman to stick in a pie: in *The Good Huswife's Jewell* he recommended boning the bird, boiling it, larding it, then enclosing in a pastry 'coffin'. The seventeenth-century recipes left behind by Sir Kenelm Digby – a courtier, diplomat, privateer, sealing wax seller, natural philosopher, astrologer and gastronome – were even more adventurous. One, entitled 'to souce turkeys', involved a boned turkey being boiled in wine and vinegar, seasoned with salt, covered with more vinegar and then stored for a month, while another required the meat to be salted for ten days before being pickled with mace and nutmeg.

Mere decades after their arrival on these shores, in an extreme example of 'taking coals to Newcastle', domesticated turkeys were being carried back across the Atlantic by migrants heading from England to the nascent colonies of North America, despite the entire continent being packed solid with wild turkeys. English settlers took turkeys with them to Virginia in 1584, an act considered by experts to be a wise one. Richard Hakluyt's *The Principall Navigations, Voiages, Traffiques and Discoveries of the English Nation* (1589) contained within it a list of essentials that transatlantic voyagers should carry. As well as dried peas, prunes and three types of cider, these included 'turkies, male and female'.

Those who followed Hakluyt's advice and kept a pair of greedy turkeys fed and watered on the long journey across the ocean may have been somewhat taken aback by what they found upon arrival. Francis Higginson, an English Puritan minister who led a group of settlers to Massachusetts in 1629, wrote in his diary: 'Here are likewise aboundance of turkies often killed in the woods, farre greater then our English turkies, and exceeding fat, sweet and fleshy, for here they have aboundance of feeding all the yeere long.' The wild North American birds were much bigger than their domesticated European cousins – there are accounts of specimens weighing as much as sixty pounds, which even allowing for the intrinsic hyperbole of hunters suggests they were vast in size – and hugely bountiful. Among numerous accounts of the birds' bewildering plenitude, Georges-Henri-Victor Collot, a French military officer who travelled through the Midwest in the eighteenth century, described seeing wild turkeys in Ohio 'in such numbers that the trees were literally rendered grey'.

Because these wild turkeys were so fat and fearless, they proved extremely popular with hungry colonialists. Their habit of sleeping in trees, usually in the same spot every night and often in large groups, made them a ridiculously easy target for well-armed hunters. As Collot explained in vivid terms: 'They are easily to be approached and even killed; but to shoot several, it is necessary to begin with such as are on the lowest branches; the rest do not move, and the whole may be killed in succession by following this method. On the contrary, in firing among those which are at the upper part of the tree, the falling of the birds through the branches frightens the rest, and makes them take flight.'

And therein lay a problem. As early as 1672, John Josselyn, a visiting Englishman, was writing that the birds had all but vanished from New England, 'the English and the Indians having now destroyed the breed, so that tis very rare to meet with wild turkie in the woods,' – although given how Native Americans had lived in harmony with wild turkeys for millennia without the slightest hint of ecocide, Josselyn's apportioning of the blame seems a little unfair. Decade by decade, wild turkey numbers rapidly diminished, their annihilation starting on the east coast and spreading in tandem with the western progress of white settlers. By the end of the nineteenth century, the wild turkey was extinct in all but the most sparsely populated of the states. *The National Cookery Book*, published in 1876, noted that the wild turkey 'is seldom seen in the cities of the Atlantic coast; here they are only to be obtained in the severe winter weather, when they are brought in a frozen condition many hundreds of miles'. By the 1930s, their American population was estimated to be less than two hundred thousand – a staggering decline from the tens of millions that bestrode the continent prior to its colonisation, and one that has, through committed, localised conservation efforts, only recently been arrested.

In light of this carnage, it was fortunate that so many settlers had chosen to bring their seemingly superfluous domesticated turkeys with them to America. These émigré fowl communed with the continent's native inhabitants far more peacefully and productively than their owners ever would, and their assignations led to the emergence of new and distinctly American breeds such as the Blue Virginia and the American Black. Slightly dizzyingly, some of these birds would, in turn, make their way back to Europe. One Hertfordshire farmer noted in 1750 that Blue Virginia turkeys 'of the flying kind' were being kept in England alongside the common Norfolk and Suffolk varieties, while the Bronze – nineteenth-century America's most popular breed, famed for its size – would find lasting favour in England.

America's increasing reliance upon domesticated birds was bolstered further by the discovery that their un-demanding disposition and penchant for worms and insects made them useful pest controllers on the tobacco farms of the South, where the tobacco hornworm was a particularly virulent antagonist. The domesticated turkey quickly became – and remains – one of the country's most popular sources of meat. Adam Hodgson, a Liverpudlian who from 1819 spent around two years travelling through the United States, wrote: 'I do not recollect to have dined a single day, from my arrival in America till I left Virginia, without a turkey on the table; often two, in gentlemen's houses.'

The American turkey is now synonymous with the country's Thanksgiving holiday, an association whose roots are not quite as deep as most Americans would have you believe. In the popular imagination, this family feast day is the continuation of a tradition dating back to the 'first thanksgiving' – a feast in 1621 at which the Pilgrim Fathers, a year after their arrival in America, marked a successful harvest by stuffing their faces with turkey. There is, however, no evidence that such a dinner took place – nor is it likely to have done, given that Puritans were famously disinclined towards fun. In the seventeenth and eighteenth centuries, Thanksgiving days were proclaimed throughout the American colonies, but these had no common date – rather, they might mark a specific event such as a military victory or a good harvest – and were as likely to involve a long day of worship as a big night of banqueting.

In Georgia in 1732, a 'plentiful' Thanksgiving dinner enjoyed by recently arrived settlers included the consumption of eight turkeys, and in the latter half of the eighteenth century, the bird became an increasingly ubiquitous part of similar spreads throughout the country. In 1806, William Bentley, a New England pastor, observed that 'a Thanksgiving is not complete without a turkey'. It was only after the end of the Civil War in 1865 that a nation crying out for the healing salve of a shared foundation myth began to promote the idea that the festival could be traced back to that fabled turkey-based blowout in Plymouth, Massachusetts. By the 1880s, Turkey Day was being used as a synonym for Thanksgiving, and romanticised depictions of hardy pilgrims tucking into turkey legs were feeding America's burgeoning sense of identity.

Back in the Pilgrim Fathers' country of birth, the turkey remained a popular but far less commonplace fowl. From as early as the 1570s, the centre for British turkey breeding had become firmly established in Norfolk and Suffolk, counties with a history of poultry rearing and an abundance of arable land whose output included large quantities of buckwheat and turnip, both ideal fodder crops. In the 1720s, in a journalistic work entitled *A Tour Thro' the Whole Island of Great Britain*, Daniel Defoe, author of *Robinson Crusoe*, reported: 'This county of Suffolk is particularly famous for furnishing the city of London, and all the counties round, with turkeys; and that tis thought, there are more turkeys bred in this county, and the part of Norfolk that adjoins to it, than in all the rest of England, especially for sale.'

Getting turkeys from the farms of East Anglia to the busy markets of London wasn't easy. This isn't a bird whose meat benefits from hanging around for long, so in the era before refrigeration, turkeys had to be transported live and, given how few could fit in a cart, predominantly on foot. This led to the surreal sight of massive gangs of fat turkeys waddling along the highways and byways of East Anglia and Essex through autumn and early winter, feeding on the post-harvest stubble of the farms that lined the route. Defoe reported that 'three hundred droves of turkeys (for they drive them all in droves on foot) pass in one season over Stratford Bridge on the River Stour'. With an average drove numbering five hundred birds, this meant that a hundred and fifty thousand turkeys could be seen toddling along this narrow road over the course of a few months. And you think the A12 is congested now.

The turkey's association with Christmas began to develop soon after the bird's arrival on these shores. There was an easy logic to this relationship: turkeys hatch in late spring and grow to full maturity in around seven months, meaning that they're ready for the dinner table in December, right on cue. In Thomas Tusser's 1573 poem *Five Hundred Pointes of Good Husbandrie*, which contains instructions for country living – like Hugh Fearnley-Whittingstall in rhyming couplets – the perfect Christmas fare was said to include: 'Beef, mutton, and pork, shred pies of the best / Pig, veal, goose, and capon, and turkey well drest.' Hannah Glasse's *The Art of Cookery* (1747) contained a recipe for 'Yorkshire Christmas pie' – a staggering construction that firmly contradicted that county's reputation for miserliness by somehow accommodating a turkey, a fowl, a partridge and a pigeon, all arranged (presumably stuffed one inside the other) 'so it will look only like a whole turkey,' then surrounded by a jointed hare, 'woodcocks, more game, and what sort of wild fowl you can get,' before being doused with 'at least four pounds of butter' and covered in pastry.

Like so much of our 'traditional' festive iconography, it was during the reign of Queen Victoria that turkeys became fundamental to the British image of Yuletide. The final chapter of Charles Dickens's phenomenally successful *A Christmas Carol* played its part in cementing the connection. Overwhelmed by his discovery of the joys of generosity, Scrooge buys a 'prize turkey' to send to the downtrodden Bob Cratchit as a gift. The former miser's excitement upon buying it borders on the unhinged: '"I shall love it, as long as I live!" cried Scrooge, patting it with his hand. "I scarcely ever looked at it before. What an honest expression it has in its face! It's a wonderful knocker! Here's the turkey. Hallo! Whoop! How are you! Merry Christmas!"'

Turkeys soon became a staple of Christmas cards and magazine illustrations, but it was only in the 1950s that they started to show up with quite the same ubiquity on Britain's festive dinner tables. The reason for this disparity was simple: cost. Domesticated turkeys proved expensive to raise, thanks in part to their hearty appetites – the sixteenth-century French scientist Charles Estienne described them as 'coffers to cast oats into; a devouring gulf of meat,' – and in part to their susceptibility to disease, harsh weather and predators. Plus, according to William Ellis, an eighteenth-century farmer from Hertfordshire, stinging nettles: 'A nettle will sting them to death, by making their head to swell, till they pine and die.' Mrs Beeton described the turkey as 'one of the most difficult birds to rear,' and claimed that 'in the middle of the eighteenth century, scarcely ten out of twenty young turkeys lived'. As a result, turkey remained an expensive bird consumed only on special occasions by the middle classes, and only dreamt of by the poor. In the twentieth century, two interlinked strands of innovation – selective breeding and intensive farming – dramatically increased the affordability of turkey, but at a high cost to the welfare of the birds, the once exalted flavour of their meat and the viability of the traditional small-scale farmers who had previously reared them.

In previous centuries, turkey breeders had tended to pay most attention to the colour and splendour of their birds' plumage, hence the emphasis given to the feathers' tone – black, white, bronze, red – in the naming of breeds. As changes in the shopping environment led to a growing likelihood that the birds would be slaughtered and plucked long before any consumer clapped eyes on them, such aesthetics became less relevant and the quantity of meat on the carcass of far greater significance. One of the first to grasp this was Jesse Throssel, an English farmer who moved to Canada in 1926 and the next year imported three Bronze turkeys from back home to use as the basis for a breeding programme focused on optimising meat content. His birds, eye-popping in the scale of their chests, were exhibited in 1930 at the Portland International Livestock Show, across the border in Oregon, and were picked up by excited American breeders who worked to further enhance these characteristics. This new breed, known as the Broad-breasted Bronze, was so wide of breast and short of leg that mating was seriously problematic, making artificial insemination a necessity, but its commercial appeal was obvious. In the 1950s, crossbreeding with the White Holland led to the development of the Broad-breasted White, which had the benefit of maturing even younger and looking neater after plucking, despite tasting of pretty much nothing. The Broad-breasted White, which sacrificed flavour for size and cheapness, now dominates large-scale turkey production in Britain and the United States.

In parallel to the ascendency of this industrial-sized bird, further efficiencies were found through the widespread adoption of cage systems. By tightly packing their turkeys into indoor pens and stuffing them with carefully formulated feed, farmers were able to produce meat with staggering efficiency, particularly after the discovery of vitamin D in 1922 allowed for the creation of supplements to eradicate rickets, a disease caused by a lack of sunlight. Today, intensively farmed turkeys are routinely de-beaked, de-toed and de-snooded within days of hatching in order to restrain the violent and often cannibalistic instincts triggered by imprisonment; they are injected with antibiotics and pumped full of high-nutrient foods; then, after a short, stressful and tedious life, they are slaughtered and automatically de-feathered.

These farming techniques, and the dominance of the Broad-breasted White, have turned mass-produced turkey into a bland shadow of the delicious bird that got Scrooge all misty-eyed. In recent years, though, Britain has seen a small but significant revival in demand for older, more flavoursome breeds, distinctive in colour and flavour, raised outdoors on a natural diet, resulting in meat that is similar in style and taste to the birds that had Thomas Tusser rhyming. These are the real prize turkeys – good enough to make the greatest of humbugs hallo and whoop; perhaps even good enough to be fed by the dozen to an Aztec emperor's menagerie.

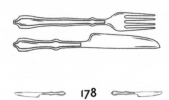

TEA

GEORGE ORWELL, WHOSE WRITING BLAZED a light
upon the social conditions and political failings of
mid-twentieth-century Britain, applied his formidable mind
to all the most pressing questions of his day: the plight of
the working poor, the evils of fascism, the dark contradic-
tions at the heart of Soviet communism. And whether it's
acceptable to put sugar in tea.

In a 1946 newspaper article, Orwell attacked the
pro-sugar camp with studied fury. 'How can you call yourself a true tea lover if you destroy the flavour of your tea
by putting sugar in it?' he wrote. 'It would be equally
reasonable to put in pepper or salt. Tea is meant to be
bitter, just as beer is meant to be bitter. If you sweeten it,
you are no longer tasting the tea, you are merely tasting
the sugar; you could make a very similar drink by dissolving
sugar in plain hot water.'

In Britain, as Orwell understood, tea really matters. It is,
in his words, 'one of the mainstays of civilisation in this
country'. And yet, notwithstanding the recent efforts of a
few ambitious pioneers in Cornwall and the Scottish
Highlands, it has never been grown on these shores in
commercially viable quantities. The bitter brew beloved of

Orwell and his countrymen is made from the leaves and leaf buds of an evergreen shrub called *Camellia sinensis*, which until the twentieth century had never been successfully cultivated on any continent other than Asia. Both the plant and the drink originated in China. The Chinese Emperor Shennong was said to have made the first brew in 2737 BCE when some stray leaves blew into his cup of boiling water – a story whose credibility is undermined by claims that he also sported a transparent stomach and single-handedly invented agriculture.

The oldest surviving reference to tea – and one that implied it was both an everyday drink and a manufactured commodity – appeared in a humorous poem by Wang Bao, who worked at the court of the Emperor Xuan. *Tong Yue* ('slave's contract'), written around 59 BCE, consisted of a long list, set out in rhyme, of the duties demanded from a recently purchased and rather peevish new slave. These included an instruction to buy tea from the market in the Sichuan town of Wuyang and prepare it for his master.

The first great treatise on tea, *Cha Jing* (c.760 CE), was written in Tang Dynasty China. In it, the scholar (and, according to some accounts, former circus clown) Lu Yu provided a practical and often poetic guide to the growing, processing and consumption of the national drink, covering everything from the appearance of the leaves ('some look like the wrinkles of a barbarian's leather boots, while others are like the bigger folds of a cow's neck,') to differences in quality ('those people who think the shiny black and smooth-looking teas are the top ones have no ability to distinguish fine tea; those who think that good tea should look yellowish with uneven wrinkles or folds have better taste,') and the best water to use ('spring water is the best, river water is second and well water is the worst'). It's a book whose blend of passionate advocacy, nerdish detail and slightly contemptuous connoisseurship feels remarkably modern, with Lu Yu's complaint that tea infused with onion, ginger, dates, orange peel, dogwood or mint tastes 'not unlike the swill of drains and ditches, and yet, alas, many people are accustomed to drinking it,' redolent of the howls of a hipster cafe owner despairing at the public's proclivity for milk and two sugars.

In Lu Yu's China, the fresh leaves were steamed, compressed into small cakes, dry-roasted, then crushed to create a powder, which was sealed in paper envelopes to preserve its fragrance. To make the drink, slightly salted water was heated to the point at which 'strings of pearls arise at the edge,' then stirred with a stick to create a whirlpool, whereupon the powder was added and the water heated further until 'the bubbles are much bigger and waves of water resound like drumming'. The tea, he wrote, should be stirred 'gracefully and smoothly,' then shared between no more than three bowls.

The Chinese love of tea made from pulverised bricks whipped up in hot water was gradually replaced by a preference for loose-leaf teas steeped in a pot. Most of these were green teas: after being picked, the leaves are quickly steamed or parched before they can oxidise, locking in the more delicate flavours and fragrances. The rest – including the variety known as oolong – were semi-oxidised through the controlled exposure of the leaves to the sun and wind, resulting in a darker colour and less subtle flavour but a longer shelf-life, better suited to transport and trade.

The old Chinese style of tea did, however, find a permanent home across the Sea of Japan. In the early ninth century,

Japanese monks began returning from China with new ideas about Buddhism and beverages. In the centuries that followed, finely milled tea powder would embed itself thoroughly in Japanese culture, becoming inexorably imbued with social and ceremonial significance. Jan Huyghen van Linschoten, a sixteenth-century Dutch merchant, wrote with utter astonishment about the Japanese love of 'warme water' and a 'certaine herb called chaa'. He was surprised not only that gentlemen were expected to personally prepare tea for their guests, but that the vessels used in its creation were so clearly venerated, despite the apparent simplicity of their construction. He explained that 'the pots wherein they sieth it, and wherein the herb is kept, with the earthen cups which they drinke it in, they esteeme as much of them, as we do of diamants, rubies and other precious stones, and they are not esteemed for their newnes but their oldnes, and for that they were made by a good workman'.

Van Linschoten's wasn't the first story about this invigorating Asian herb to catch the attention of Europeans. One widely read account from 1559, written by the Venetian magistrate Giovanni Battista Ramusio, who collated the journals of the era's most adventurous explorers and helped bring them to a mass audience, recounted a conversation he'd had with a Persian trader, Chaggi Memet, 'a man of great talent and judgement' who had been in Venice – then the unrivalled hub of European trade with the east – for several months pushing a large consignment of dried rhubarb. Rhubarb root, a traditional Chinese medicine, was then a valuable commodity in Europe and the Levant, transported along the spice routes by Muslim merchants and bought at great expense by wealthy westerners. The worldly Persian told Ramusio how the people of China also 'make use of another plant, or rather its leaves,' drunk 'as hot as can be tolerated'. Such was their love of this invigorating infusion, known as 'chiai', the Chinese would happily swap 'a sack of rhubarb' for just one ounce. Chaggi provided a downbeat and highly prophetic forecast for the future of his hitherto thriving trade: the Chinese had told him that if tea 'was known in our parts, and in Persia and the land of the Franks, merchants would, without doubt, no longer want to buy [rhubarb]'. The global tea market is currently worth around $50 billion per year, the global rhubarb root market somewhat less.

Portuguese sailors brought tea back to Europe in the early seventeenth century, but only in tiny quantities and with no great purpose beyond the sharing of an Oriental novelty. The first Europeans to establish a regular trade were the Dutch. In January 1637, the board of the Dutch East India Company – then the dominant European trading entity in Asia – wrote to the Governor-General in Jakarta, Indonesia, with an instruction that suggested that European interest in tea had reached a tipping point, making it commercially useful: 'As the tea begins to come into use with some people, we expect some jars of Chinese as well as Japanese tea with all ships.' In the Netherlands, this expensive new import initially proved divisive, treated with reverence by some and disdainfully dismissed by others as *heu wasser* ('hay water'), but the profits accrued in the European markets quickly expunged any doubts.

In the 1650s, Dutch tea imports began appearing on the menus of London's coffeehouses, advertised as a healthy brew. In 1658, the republican magazine *Mercurius Politicus* announced: 'That excellent and by all physitians approved China drink, called by the Chinese tcha, by other nations tay, alias tee, is sold at the Sultaness Head, a cophee-house in Sweetings Rents, by the Royal Exchange, London.' Just as it remains today, seventeenth-century London was a city in which new fashions came roaring to life, so, like coffee and chocolate before it, tea quickly became a firm favourite among the chattering classes. The civil servant and diarist Samuel Pepys, an excellent barometer of social fads, tried his first cup in September 1660 after visiting the office to talk with colleagues about the benefits of a good war with France or Holland: 'And afterwards I did send for a cup of tee (a China drink) of which I never had drank before, and went away.' Pepys would later note how the 'potticary' Mr Pelling had told Mrs Pepys that drinking tea would be 'good for her cold and defluxions'. The marriage of Charles II to the tea-loving Portuguese princess Catherine of Braganza in 1662 added to the drink's glamour – a rather unctuous poem by Edward Waller praised her as 'the best of Queens' and tea as 'the best of herbs', one which will 'regress those vapours which the head invade, / And keep the palace of the soul serene'.

Sir Kenhelm Digby explained how a 'Jesuite that came from China' in 1664 had offered some advice to novice drinkers: 'In these parts, he saith, we let the hot water remain too long soaking upon the tea, which makes it extract into itself the earthy parts of the herb. The water is to remain upon it, no longer that whiles you can say the Miserere Psalm very leisurely.' Digby's contact also recommended a use for tea that sounds, quite frankly, vile: 'To near a pint of the infusion, take two yolks of new laid-eggs, and beat them very well with as much fine sugar as is sufficient for this quantity of liquor; when they are very well incorporated, pour your tea upon the eggs and sugar, and stir them well together. So drink it hot. This is when you come home from attending business abroad, and are very hungry, and yet have not conveniency to eat presently a competent meal.' Given the drink's novelty, expert instruction could certainly be useful. As one essayist recounted: 'It is related, upon good authority, that in 1685, the widow of the unfortunate Duke of Monmouth sent a pound of tea as a present to some of her noble relations in Scotland; but having omitted to send the needful directions for its use, the tea was boiled, the liquor thrown away, and the leaves served up at table as a vegetable.' At least they didn't deep-fry it.

In those early decades, most of the shipments to Britain were of green tea, but as the eighteenth century progressed, the scales increasingly tipped towards hardier semi-oxidised forms, which didn't need to be treated with quite the same care. Teas were named and graded using Anglicised corruptions of Chinese words: the cheapest was bohea, with its dark, robust and rather harsh leaves; congou, souchong and pekoe were also semi-oxidised, but were of progressively higher quality; singlo was common green tea; while the posher greens were known initially as bing, then later as hyson. Britain's increasing access to cheap sugar grown by slaves in the Caribbean colonies played a significant role in shaping the growing British demand for cheap bohea, offering as it did a means of rendering even the roughest of brews more palatable – from the very start, tea and sugar were seen as natural bedfellows, as were tea and sugary foods.

It wasn't until the early twentieth century, when changes in the dairy industry made milk more readily available, allowing its mellowing effect on harsh, cheap leaves to come to the fore, that milky tea became part of British culture. It did, though, have a precedent in the drink's homeland. In the 1650s, Johan Nieuhof, part of a Dutch delegation to the court of the Qing emperor, wrote of the preference for milky tea among the Manchu, the northern Chinese people who in 1644 had toppled the once-mighty Ming dynasty. After a lavish reception in the port town of Canton (Guangzhou), at which tea was served at the start of the dinner, Nieuhof joked that 'the Chinese boast as much of the excellency of this infusion, as the alchemists of the vertues of their pretended elixir,' and explained that the Manchu habit was to 'add warm milk, about a fourth part, with a little salt'. Nieuhof said that this use of milk was 'not so well approved' by other Chinese ethnic groups, who preferred their tea served straight or with a touch of sugar – an early hint of the scorn currently directed toward chai lattes by all right-thinking people.

Nieuhof was broadly accepting of his hosts' claims as to the many health benefits of tea – in particular, he noted having encountered no one in China suffering from 'stone or gout', conditions endured by many hard-drinking Europeans. He wasn't alone in this judgement. In 1678, another Dutchman, Cornelis Bontekoe, published his *Treatise about the Most Excellent Herb Tea*, an influential tract that recommended the daily consumption of a stag-gering quantity of tea, which he claimed would warm and thin the blood with near miraculous consequences for health and wellbeing. In 1680s London, Thomas Povey, a founding fellow of the Royal Society, listed twenty qualities associated with tea, clearly inspired by the work of Bontekoe. Some of these sound useful but essentially mundane ('purifies defects of the bladder and kiddneys.' 'prevents the dropsie,' 'drives away all the paines of the collick which proceed from wind'); others, slightly more surreal in their phrasing, are unlikely to make their way into a PG Tips ad campaign any time soon ('easeth the brain of heavy damps,' 'vanquisheth heavy dreams,' 'consumes rawnesse').

Not everyone was convinced. John Wesley, the founder of Methodism, claimed in 1748 that the drink had caused in him a 'paralytick disorder', and counselled abstinence from this 'deadly poison'. Jonas Hanway, a merchant made famous in the 1750s by his travel writing, went even further, claiming that not only was tea making the British ill, it was making them ugly: 'Men seem to have lost their stature and comeliness; and women their beauty . . . methinks there is not quite so much beauty in this land as there was.' The lexicographer and intellectual brawler Samuel Johnson, who hated foolishness almost as much as he loved a cuppa, fought back in a series of diatribes that demolished Hanway's flimsy science. Johnson called himself 'a hardened and shameless tea-drinker, who has for twenty years diluted his meals with only the infusion of this fascinating plant; whose kettle has scarcely time to cool; who with tea amuses the evening, with tea solaces the midnight, and with tea welcomes the morning'. As well as standing up for the enduring beauty of Britain's womenfolk, regardless of their choice of hot beverage, Johnson identified the growing social importance of tea, claiming that drinkers are 'brought together not by the tea, but the teatable'.

* * *

By then, the principal importer of this increasingly popular drink was the East India Company, whose royal charter gave it a monopoly on British trade with the Far East and whose enthusiastic embrace of the tea trade responded to – and helped fuel – the surge in British demand. Its first shipments arrived in 1669, weighing a total of one hundred and forty-three pounds; by the end of the seventeenth century, annual imports averaged just short of thirty-seven thousand pounds; in 1724, the weight of Company tea consumed in Britain surpassed the million-pound mark for the first time. As tea's popularity and profitability swelled, so too did the British government's eagerness to tax it, using a highly regressive measure based on weight rather than price. By 1745, duties on cheap tea amounted to around one hundred and twenty per cent of the net cost. The inevitable consequence of this ill-judged fiscal gouging was a tidal wave of shameless smuggling, with black-market tea flooding onto isolated British beaches from Denmark, Sweden, the Netherlands and France (tea of better quality, too, as unlike the East India Company, which favoured bohea, continental merchants tended to only deal in the primo stuff). Large criminal enterprises were soon making vast fortunes from this unlikely contraband, the most notorious being the Hawkhurst Gang, which operated along much of the south coast, honing the classic mafia tropes of intimidation, patronage and gruesome murder.

The high taxes on tea particularly aggrieved the citizens of Britain's American colonies, who were already deeply unhappy with the fiscal burden imposed by London. Overpriced East India Company tea became a powerful symbol of British perfidy. As Abraham Lott, a New York merchant and patriot, wrote: 'The people would rather buy so much poison, as they say it is calculated to enslave them and their posterity, and are therefore determined not to take what they call the nauseous draught.' At the Boston Tea Party of 1773, hundreds of chests of tea were dumped in the harbour by protestors – a moment of great symbolism in the slow brewing of the American revolution.

In 1784, William Pitt took the sensible step of cutting the duty on tea down to the bone and instead taxing windows, which are far harder to hide from the taxman. The following year, demand for legitimate East India Company tea brought into sharp relief just how comically massive the scale of the black market must have been. In 1783, just over three million pounds of tea was sold by the Company for domestic consumption. Two years later, the figure was just over thirteen million pounds.

In less than a century and a half, tea had become a commodity with a truly national reach. In 1801, the East India Company clerk Robert Wissett wrote: '[Tea] may be literally said to have descended from the palace to the cottage, and from a fashionable and expensive luxury, has been converted into an essential comfort, if not an absolute necessity of life.' David Davies, a tea trader based close to Borough Market, told a parliamentary select committee in 1834: 'Almost everyone uses tea – that is, no one, scarcely, goes without tea at least once a day.' More than any other drink, tea transcended wealth and status, leaping the often impassable social barriers of this most class-bound of nations and burying itself deep into the rhythms and rituals of rich and poor alike – the stately high tea, the factory tea break, the simple evening meal still known throughout the north of England as 'tea'. As Samuel Phillips Day wrote in 1878: 'The artist at his easel, the author at his desk, the statesman fresh from an exhaustive oration, the actor from the stage after fulfilling an arduous role, the orator from the platform, the preacher from the pulpit, the toiling mechanic, the wearied labourer, the poor governess, the tired laundress, the humble cottage housewife, the votary of pleasure even, on escaping from the scene of revelry, nay, the Queen on her throne, have, one and all, to acknowledge and express gratitude for the grateful and invigorating infusion.' Even the utterly destitute would often favour tea over food. According to George Orwell: 'Unemployment is an endless misery that has got to be constantly palliated, and especially with tea, the Englishman's opium.'

In the decade before 1784, the East India Company sold around twenty-eight per cent of the tea imported to Europe; in the 1790s, it handled seventy-eight per cent of the almost three hundred billion pounds of tea that headed west from China. Since 1757, as part of China's determined effort to keep western traders where it could see them, the entire trade had been restricted to the port city of Canton, and all tea purchased there had to be paid for in gold, silver or copper, the Chinese having maintained an entirely reasonable refusal to accept in exchange the second-rate consumer goods that underpinned European trade elsewhere in the world. In order to get its hands on the necessary precious metals to keep the money train rolling, the East India Company's ruse was to load up on Indian opium – the supply of which it controlled – and sell it illicitly in China via a network of agents, a model tacitly supported by the British government. The European appetite for tea and the

Chinese appetite for opium became inextricably interlinked, with the British managing to profit from both strands. When in 1839 the Chinese began to suppress the opium trade, which was destroying the country's trade balance and ruining the lives of millions of addicts, the Royal Navy intervened with some of its signature gunboat diplomacy, sparking the Opium Wars. British success in the conflict – a war *for* drugs, rather than the now familiar, and far less successful, war *on* drugs – led to Hong Kong being ceded to the victors and Chinese ports being opened up to the unrestricted sale of opium and tea, thus tightening Britain's grip on the global tea trade still further.

By then, though, the East India Company's dominance of the Chinese tea market was already coming to an end. In 1834, with consensus building around the benefits of free trade, the Company's monopoly on traffic between China and Britain was brought to an end by Parliament. As competition flourished, traders were incentivised to build ever faster ships to bring the new season's tea back from China. Beautiful, streamlined tea clippers began racing across the oceans in search of the highest prices at market. With its revenues severely threatened, the East India Company's response was to explore the idea of setting up tea plantations in India, a country that the Company, a private enterprise with its own army and civil servants, ran on behalf of the British government.

A decade earlier, in Assam, north-eastern India, the Scottish explorer Robert Bruce had stumbled upon forests filled with an indigenous variety of wild tea (local people had, of course, discovered it much earlier, using its leaves to make pickles as well as drinks), and the Company poured its efforts into exploiting the possibilities presented by this native plant. Soon, vast swathes of the region's vegetation were being cleared to accommodate a profitable new monoculture, and forms of indentured servitude were imposed upon local inhabitants to feed its rapacious need for labour. Cultivated Assam tea leaves, which were first sold in London in January 1839, were larger and coarser than their delicate Chinese cousins, and the resulting drink was malty and bracing, but that did little to put off the sugar-loving British. By 1888, more tea was being exported to the UK from Assam than from China, a remarkable turnaround in just a few decades.

While the Assam tea boom was getting underway, the East India Company was, in parallel, attempting to introduce more desirable and sophisticated Chinese plants to India. Such efforts had always previously failed, mainly due to a lack of knowledge on the part of the British, but in 1851, another Scotsman, Robert Fortune, managed to smuggle thousands of young tea plants and – perhaps more importantly – eight expert tea growers from China to the Company's Indian plantations. Some of these plants ended up in the mountainous region of Darjeeling, where they flourished. Supported by a perfect blend of rich, loamy soil, sunshine and cool Himalayan winds, the offspring of those illegally transplanted bushes evolved into something distinctive: Chinese in origin but specific in character to the region that had become their home. First-flush Darjeeling now bears comparison with the finest teas of China, Japan and Korea.

The uncanny ability of Scotsmen to transform international tea production did not end with Bruce and Fortune. In 1904, Arnold Butler McDonell bought a parcel of land in Kenya as part of a British initiative to persuade white settlers to begin farming in the East African colony. He attempted to grow coffee, corn and flax, but none of the crops took. Then, in 1918, a friend sent him some Assam tea seedlings from India and the resulting bushes began to thrive in the sunny, mountainous terrain. Eight years later, McDonell opened the country's first commercial tea-processing factory. Now, Kenya is the largest exporter of tea to the UK, and tea plantations dominate the country's sunny uplands. Most is still harvested manually, making it an important source of local employment, but the larger plantations tend to be owned by massive western corporations whose profits do little to improve life in East Africa.

The tea drunk in Britain today is mostly black tea, a version even more dark and astringent than the cheap bohea of old, made by 'withering' the leaves, then rolling or kneading them until they fully oxidise – a process born of the paucity of skill among the first British growers in India, who lacked the know-how to make semi-oxidised tea. The Chinese started making black tea in the nineteenth century, but only to sell to westerners, and very few Japanese would allow such a drink to darken their palate either, unless out of politeness to a European host. Nor have either of these great tea cultures embraced Britain's other industrial innovation: in 1931, Sir William McKercher, superintendent of the Amgoorie Tea Estate in Assam, developed the 'crush-tear-curl' system of manufacturing, which used powerful machinery to process the leaves, negating the need for skilled labourers and resulting in a tea with a much finer grain. This black, bitter and decidedly unsubtle preparation is well suited to the kind of quick infusion required of teabags, and a variant on crush-tear-curl continues to dominate the south Asian and African tea plantations that supply the UK.

The concept of creating submergible bags of tea in individual portions blossomed at the start of the twentieth century in the natural home of individualism: the USA. There are many claimants to the idea, none of them entirely convincing, but whoever's idea it was, by the middle of the century over a third of the tea consumed in America came in this form, which offered both convenience and frugality – a single bag can make a decent brew from the dustiest of low-grade teas without muddying the drink. The first British company to jump on the bandwagon was Tetley, which introduced its bags to a deeply sceptical nation in 1953. Uptake was slow, but by 1972, teabags accounted for sixteen per cent of tea sales. Now, that percentage is comfortably in the nineties. Teabags changed the nature of the tea we drink and also the way we drink it, turning its preparation from a slow, communal ritual based around a pot into a quicker and more solitary experience.

Despite all the changes in both production and consumption, tea remains our national drink. In recent years, with coffee-drinking making giant strides, its hegemony has declined somewhat, but the UK remains third on the list of per capita tea consumption (Turkey is out in front, Ireland number two). It's still of huge cultural importance. And George Orwell is still right about sugar.

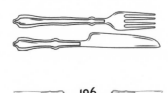

STRAWBERRIES

I N HIS BOOK *THE COMPLEAT Angler* (1653–55), Izaak Walton, the writer and celebrity trout fisherman, made passing reference to the thoughts of Dr William Butler – a sixteenth-century court physician, drunkard and inventor of the dubious-sounding Dr Butler's Purging Ale – regarding the rightful place of the strawberry in the pantheon of fruits. 'Doubtless God could have made a better berry,' Butler is reported to have said, 'but doubtless God never did.'

Many people today – with the strawberry firmly established as a totem of our national cuisine, as emblematic of the English summertime as Ashes defeats, crowded pub gardens and untimely drizzle – would be eager to agree with the good doctor's assessment of the fruit, even if they wouldn't be quite so keen to sample his beer. But in Butler's day, this veneration of the strawberry was not widely shared, particularly by those in the upper echelons of society. And while the eagerness with which we consume these berries has expanded considerably (as have the fruits themselves), their success cannot be easily attributed to God. Instead, modern strawberries are a prime example of mankind's ability, through a combination of happy accident and creative design, to mould nature to suit our own evolving tastes.

Wild strawberries of various shapes and sizes have been foraged across much of the planet for thousands of years. These include three native European species, of which the wood strawberry (*Fragaria vesca*) managed to spread itself most widely, while the musk strawberry (*Fragaria moschata*) and the green strawberry (*Fragaria viridis*) remained rather more obscure. Various distinctive local subspecies of the wood strawberry also evolved, including the visually striking white strawberry and the highly vigorous Alpine variety, which bears its flowers and elegantly elongated fruit for the full length of the summer.

None of these were widely revered in the ancient world – or at least not by the kind of people who wrote about such things. Strawberries were overlooked by many of the great Greek and Roman naturalists, from Hippocrates and Dioscorides to Varro and Columella. Pliny the Elder mistakenly believed the fruit to be 'kindred' to the arbutus tree (they look very much alike, despite being unrelated) and given his countrymen's disdain for arbutus berries, which were 'held in no esteem . . . people being generally content with eating but one,' this was not a favourable association. In *The Natural History,* he included the strawberry in a chapter about 'plants that grow spontaneously' and are 'employed as an aliment by most nations,' but which, his tone suggested, were not of any great importance. The rest of the list consisted of such obscurities as 'the tamnus, the butcher's broom, the sea batis, and the garden batis,' as well as 'the meadow parsnip and the hop, which may be rather termed amusements for the botanist than articles of food,' – definitely not good company for any ambitious foodstuff to be keeping.

The strawberry was thoroughly ignored by the Roman *De Re Coquinaria* cookbook and was absent too from the great European culinary tomes of the medieval period – *The Forme of Cury, Le Viandier, Liber de Coquina* – none of which contained a single mention. One Anglo-Norman manuscript produced in Hereford in the first half of the fourteenth century included within a short selection of recipes a sweet dish called 'fryseye' – strawberries softened in almond milk, thickened with rice flour or amidon (starch), mixed with coarse meat, cinnamon and sugar, dyed with red colouring, then topped with more strawberries – but beyond that and a few other cursory mentions, the fruit maintained a strangely liminal presence: clearly common-place and doubtless consumed in big sticky handfuls by anyone who found themselves wandering hungry through the woodlands of Europe, yet almost entirely ignored by those blessed with power and literacy.

Why, then, given that wild strawberries are unquestion-ably delicious – their Latin name, *fraga*, meant sweet-smelling – were they so undervalued? In part, their very wildness seems to have been a problem. Unlike apples, pears, figs, grapes and cherries, all of which were cultivated in the ancient world and propagated through the rippling cross-continental flow of trade and conquest, strawberries were a fruit of the forest, not of the orchard. The Roman poet Ovid described them in his *Metamorphoses* (8 CE) as a food of the 'golden age' – a romanticised version of pre-agricultural life: 'The teeming Earth, yet guiltless of the plough, / And unprovok'd, did fruitful stores allow: / Content with food, which Nature freely bred, / On wildings and on strawberries they fed.'

Since the dawn of civilisation, most cultures have held those foods that are produced by people in higher esteem than those foraged from the wilderness – and however sweet they may taste, Europe's wild strawberry species have never been particularly well suited to cultivation. The fruits of the wood strawberry family are small and somewhat sparse (the 'vesca' part of its taxonomic name means thin or weak), making them awkward and inefficient as a food crop. And although the musk strawberry offers pleasingly plump berries, the plants are dioecious, meaning that each one has only male or female characteristics: both a male and a female are required for reproduction, but only the female will bear fruit. Anyone attempting to cultivate musk strawberries is required to retain some of the seemingly sterile bushes as well as the attractively fruit-laden ones for there to be any hope of future propagation – by no means an intuitive act.

The manner in which wild strawberries hang so low to the ground also sullied their reputation. Virgil, another Roman poet, was concerned about the health and safety implications of picking them – in his *Declogue* (c.44–38 BCE), he wrote: 'You, picking flowers and strawberries that grow / So near the ground, fly hence, boys, get you gone! / There's a cold adder lurking in the grass.' In the twelfth century, Hildegard of Bingen insisted that the berries are 'not good to eat for either the healthy or the sick, because they grow close to the earth and because they even grow in foul air'. As well as putting people off eating them, the inclination of the fruit-bearing runners to spread along the floor informed the English name of the plant, with the Anglo-Saxon root of the word being the same as that of the verb to 'strew'.

Hildegard, one of the most influential theologians of her

era, may have decried the strawberry's suitability as a food-stuff, but its place within the complex carapace of religious symbolism was generally a positive one. With its red heart-shape and the overtones of pastoral innocence, the strawberry plant and its individual berries were used by medieval painters as symbols of righteousness and modesty, frequently adorning depictions of the Virgin Mary and the infant Christ. A somewhat less innocent (but no less joyous) vision was conjured up in Hieronymus Bosch's remarkable triptych *The Garden of Earthly Delights* (c.1490–1510) – just beneath the chap with a bunch of flowers up his bottom (surely the high watermark of medieval art) is a nude man straddling a giant strawberry.

The gradual ascent in the status of the strawberry as a food only really began after a few wealthy Europeans with large gardens began transplanting wild strawberries from the woods to the terrace. In 1368, Jean Dudoy, King Charles V's gardener, planted thousands of wood strawberry plants in the royal gardens of the Louvre in Paris. The Duke of Burgundy, whose wife was apparently obsessed with the things, soon followed suit at the Château de Couvres near Dijon. The May 1530 privy purse expenses of Henry VIII, a man associated more often with the epic consumption of meat, show that his household paid money to 'Jasper of Beaulie the gardyner in reward for bringing streberyes to the king,' and William Shakespeare also alluded to the fruits being enjoyed by royalty: in *Richard III*, the future king says to the Bishop of Ely: 'When I was last in Holborn / I saw good strawberries in your garden there. / I do beseech you send for some of them.'

As well as the common wood strawberry, gardeners on English estates began experimenting with the large and intensely flavoured musk strawberry, also known as the 'hautbois' or the Bohemian – described by the botanist John Parkinson as the 'goodliest and greatest' of strawberries. Frustrating though cultivating them could be, with their unisexual nature not yet understood, the English gamely persisted. Over in France, however, the species was widely derided. Jean-Baptiste de La Quintinie, who managed the gardens at the Palace of Versailles in the seventeenth century, instructed that any musk strawberries be 'torn out, or at least that no particular friendliness be held toward them'. The French are, of course, never slow to highlight our culinary coarseness. '[The musk strawberry] has been known for a very long time in the gardens around Paris, but it is scorned there,' wrote the great French botanist Antoine Nicolas Duchesne. 'The English cultivate it, on the contrary, to adorn their tables.' The philistines.

In 1577, in *The Gardener's Labyrinth*, Thomas Hill suggested that the strawberry had become a popular fixture in the English diet when the summer months rolled around. 'They be much eaten at all men's tables in the sommer time with wine and sugar,' he wrote. Another enduring English accompaniment had also been established: Andrew Boorde, in *A Dyetary of Health* (1542), described as 'a rural man's banquet' strawberries eaten with 'raw cream undecocted,' adding that 'such banquets hath put men in jeopardy of their lives,' – although the danger, he made clear, lay with the cream, not with the strawberries. His slightly patronising reference to 'rural' people's love of strawberries and cream is, though, a telling one. Despite them being cultivated in the gardens of gentlemen, the sense that the strawberry was an unsophisticated rustic food had not gone away. Certainly, the cookbooks of Boorde's era and the two centuries that followed – tomes that offered insights into the dining habits of those wealthy families that could afford to employ cooks – gave the impression that this was a fruit still unvalued within the kitchens of the rich.

It wasn't entirely absent from the canon – there was, for example, a recipe for 'tarte of strawberry' in Thomas Dawson's *The Good Huswife's Jewell* (1585) – but its presence was marginal at best. Sir Kenelm Digby's seventeenth-century recipe collection frequently mentioned strawberry leaves being utilised as a flavouring for the alcoholic drink metheglin, but the fruit was put to use just once, in strawberry wine – at no point did Digby suggest eating one. *Mrs Mary Eales's Receipts*, first published in 1718 and attributed to the eponymous 'confectioner to her late Majesty Queen Anne', was entirely given over to sweet dishes, the vast majority of which contained fruit of some kind, but her sole mention of strawberries came in a passage about berries that are suitable for freezing in a solid-fruit sorbet. Eliza Smith's *The Compleat Housewife* (1727) also referred to them just once, in a recipe for a fool, and then only as an alternative to raspberries. Most notably, not a single strawberry adorned the pages of Hannah Glasse's vast masterpiece *The Art of Cookery* (1747) – gooseberries, raspberries, blackberries, rosehips, elderberries and redcurrants were variously used in jellies, fools, pies, sweet creams, wafers, preserves and fruit wines (lots of fruit wines), but the strawberry was nowhere to be found.

*   *   *

And there, had a remarkable sequence of events not unfolded, is where this tale might have ended, with the strawberry being cultivated in small gardens, but, like the rosehip or the gooseberry, ignored by the large-scale producers and high-street retailers who respond to – and shape – the tastes of the nation. That the strawberry would become a centrepiece of Britain's culinary culture, gobbled up by the bucket-load across every stratum of society, was by no means inevitable, and its unfolding was the result of an unlikely storyline that played itself out across three continents and several centuries.

This story – one of intellectual curiosity, hard science and a generous dollop of dumb luck – began around the same time that Hieronymus Bosch was painting a plump strawberry into the central panel of his erotic triptych. When European colonists began exploring the Americas, among the many earthly delights they encountered were two long-established American strawberry species. It was their discovery that would, before long, cause the tectonic plates of European horticulture to shift irreversibly.

The first of these plants, brought back from North America, was the Virginia strawberry (*Fragaria virginiana*), the large but rather bland fruits of which would become known in England as 'scarlets'. In 1624, an American strawberry was being described by Jean and Vespasian Robin, botanists to the French King Louis XIII. Five years later, John Parkinson made clear that the Virginia strawberry was being grown in England, too, although not very successfully. The Virginia plant 'carryeth the best leaf of any other, except the Bohemian,' he wrote, referring to the musk strawberry, 'but scarce can one strawberry be seene ripe among a number of plants'. This he put down to a 'want of skill or industry' on the part of the English.

A second American import would soon arrive in Europe to much greater fanfare. Long cultivated by the Mapuche and Huilliche Indians, the Chilean strawberry (*Fragaria chiloensis*) bore fruits of immense size. In 1646, the Jesuit missionary Alonso de Ovalle wrote of buying them in Chile: 'Although I saw them growing wild for miles, they are very expensive when cultivated. Their taste and smell differ from those I saw in Rome. In size, they are as large as pears and are mostly red, but in the territory of Concepción there are also white and yellow ones.' The journey made by this fruit from South America to Europe would lead to the transformation of our perception of the entire genus – and it was overseen by a French spy whose name was Strawberry. Honestly.

Lieutenant Colonel Amédée François Frézier was clearly born to play this part. His surname was a derivation of *fraisier*, the French word for 'strawberry plant' – a result, it was claimed, of his ancestor Julius de Berry (again, this is not a joke) feeding vast plates of the fruit to Emperor Charles the Simple in 916; to mark this auspicious occasion, the Frézier family coat of arms consisted of three strawberries hanging on their stalks.

In January 1712, Frézier, then a thirty-one-year-old engineer in the French Army Intelligence Corp, set off for Chile and Peru, posing as a merchant, to spy on the Spanish colonial fortifications and, in his words, such 'things which might hereafter be of great use to the French, if a war should happen to break out again between the two nations'. Just how useful a new variety of soft fruit would prove in such circumstances is unclear, but the French military moves in mysterious ways. Frézier described seeing stupendous strawberries growing in Concepción: 'They plant whole fields with a sort of strawberry rushes, differing from ours, in that the leaves are rounder, thicker and more downy. The fruit is generally as big as a walnut, and sometimes as a hen's egg, of a whitish red, and somewhat less delicious of taste than our wood strawberries.' In 1714, he sailed back to Marseilles with five of these alien plants in his luggage. One he kept for himself, two he left with the officer in charge of the ship's fresh water supply (a thank you, no doubt, for his voluminous and somewhat unconventional use of a valuable resource), one he gave to Pelletier de Souzy, his boss in the Ministry of Fortifications in Brest, Brittany, and one he presented to 'Monsieur de Jussieu for the King's garden, where care will be taken to bring them to bear'.

Unfortunately for Antoine de Jussieu, and for all those European botanists who couldn't wait to get their first glimpse of an egg-sized Chilean strawberry, *Fragaria chiloensis* is, like the musk strawberry, dioecious – and all five of Frézier's plants happened to be female. When selecting plants to bring back to Europe, the Frenchman had been understandably drawn to those bearing big, beautiful fruits, unaware that at least one of the dull, fruitless male plants would be needed as well. Although grafts of the Chilean plants were quickly distributed to various gardens, particularly around Brest – perhaps by De Souzy, perhaps by Frézier himself – and grew with some vigour, not a single *Fragaria chiloensis* fruit could be persuaded to appear.

In England, Philip Miller, chief gardener at the Chelsea

Physic Garden, was among those who tried and failed, having procured Chilean plants from Dutch growers who had themselves been sent runners by De Jussieu. He wrote: 'I brought some of the plants from Holland, anno 1727, which thrive and increase exceedingly, but as yet I have obtained no fruit; the last season, anno 1729, they produced great numbers of flowers, which were larger than the hautboy strawberry, in proportion to the bulk of its fruit; but I am in hopes next season to obtain some fruit in perfection.' Those hopes were in vain.

Back in France, though, some *Fragaria chiloensis* plants had begun to perform. In 1731, Miller wrote, doubtless with a touch of envy, that Chilean plants had 'produced fruit several years in the Royal Garden at Paris, where Monsieur Jussieu assured me, it was commonly as large as a small apple'. The more observant French gardeners began to notice that these successes only occurred when the exotic newcomers were planted alongside musk strawberries and Virginian strawberries. The significance of this observation would be unearthed by the greatest thinker in the history of the strawberry – a forgotten giant of the Enlightenment who would surely be more famous today had he applied his formidable intellect to a subject slightly less niche than soft summer berries.

The Isaac Newton of the strawberry was Antoine Nicolas Duchesne, author of *L'Histoire Naturelle des Fraisiers* (1766) – an extraordinary book, published when Duchesne was just nineteen years old (and it wasn't even his first scholarly work, following as it did a comprehensive survey of the characteristics of plants found around Paris, knocked out when he was seventeen). Two years earlier, in July 1764,

Duchesne, the son of a mid-ranking official at the court of Versailles, had personally presented King Louis XV with a pot of big, beautiful strawberries produced by fertilising a Chilean strawberry plant with the pollen of the musk strawberry – a combination of botanical finesse and shameless toadying that gained him unfettered access to the invaluable resources found in de Jussieu's royal gardens.

In compiling his masterpiece, the young prodigy drew upon writings and samples gathered from horticulturalists all over Europe – then, as now, scientists across the continent were remarkably close and cooperative, however fragile their nations' political relationships may have been. Among his regular correspondents was Carl Linnaeus, the father of modern taxonomy, who tolerated the far younger man's criticisms of his classification of strawberries and was impressed by his overwhelming and, in an era of polymaths, highly unusual, monomania. Linnaeus wrote: 'When you have completed the history of the wild strawberries, you will have accomplished something which I long have hoped that some botanists would do; namely, that they would each choose their plant family and examine it most thoroughly; in this manner would soon be attained the ultimate knowledge of plants which now floods botanists with its abundance.'

It was Duchesne who convincingly described ten species of strawberry and six distinct varieties of the wood strawberry. It was he who proved that the plants of several of these species – including both the musk strawberry and the Chilean – are single-sex. And it was he who demonstrated through rigorous testing that the female Chilean strawberry could be successfully pollinated by both the musk and the

Virginian, but not by the far more commonplace wood strawberry. We now know why: while Chileans and Virginians have fifty-six chromosomes each, making them perfect partners, the wood strawberry has just fourteen, hence its incompatibility. The musk strawberry has forty-two chromosomes, meaning that while it can occasionally cross with its American cousins, those crosses are themselves not productive.

It was also Duchesne who correctly posited that an entirely new species of strawberry, whose large, watery fruits carried a distinct whiff of pineapple and whose sudden appearance in gardens and markets had begun to fascinate horticulturalists (for some reason, when Philip Miller first encountered them, he was convinced they came from Surinam), was, in fact, the hybrid child of a Chilean and a Virginian. But perhaps most importantly, it was he who discovered that *Fragaria ananassa*, as this new species became known, was, unlike its frustratingly unisexual parents, a perfect hermaphrodite.

The new strawberry identified by Duchesne changed the rules of the game. *Fragaria ananassa* might have lacked some of the flavour punch of Europe's ancient natives, but it was fragrant and fat and could happily pollinate itself, with every single plant bearing fruit. It was also highly responsive to crossing and backcrossing, making it a horti-culturalist's dream. In short, this vigorous hybrid, unlike the berries of old, offered the potential for money to be made by growers – and wherever the potential for profit emerges, investment and innovation rapidly follow. Over the following couple of centuries, *Fragaria ananassa* would become completely and utterly dominant. Today, other than

a few tiny crops of wood strawberries and musk strawberries, some of which might find their way onto the menus
of serious-minded chefs who revel in sourcing obscure native
ingredients, there is barely a single strawberry consumed in
the western world that does not owe its existence to this
improbable and entirely manmade collision of two different
plant species from two different continents, transplanted
thousands of miles to a third.

In the first half of the nineteenth century, it was Britain – a
world leader in both commerce and science – that refined
the art of selectively breeding *Fragaria ananassa* (known
for a while as the 'pine strawberry' before its ubiquity
rendered any such differentiation unnecessary) to create
ever more attractive and marketable fruits. 'The wedding
ceremony of the American immigrants was celebrated in
England,' wrote Edward Bunyard in *The Anatomy of
Dessert* (1929), 'and for some years the large modern fruits
were called "English" in Continental countries.' Among the
leaders in the field were Thomas Andrew Knight, the
eminent founder of the Royal Horticultural Society, who
used a highly controlled crossing system to create the
popular Downton and Elton varieties, and Michael Keens,
a market gardener from Isleworth, who despite being far
less systematic in his approach was arguably even more
successful. The fruits of the Keens Seedling, first described
in 1821, were large and richly red, their vivid tones bleeding
into a soft white centre, and they grew both prolifically
and reliably, conveniently high from the ground (Virgil
would definitely have approved).

As the fat, fecund fruits emerging from the assiduous

work of those Victorian horticulturalists spread through the gardens of Britain, gradually replacing the underappreciated native varieties of old, their culinary appeal grew in tandem. In 1861, Mrs Beeton offered a clear indication of just how far the strawberry had come in the century since Hannah Glasse had ignored it completely. Beeton's book was awash with strawberries – eaten with cream, packed into vol-au-vents and tarts, preserved in wine or sugar, used to flavour blancmanges, jellies, ice creams and creams, or presented on a dish for a 'particularly refreshing' breakfast. Writing about the raspberry, she declared it to be not as 'universally esteemed as the strawberry, with whose lusciousness and peculiarly agreeable flavour it can bear no comparison'. And so it was, thanks to a French spy, an adolescent genius and a whole host of entrepreneurial market gardeners, that the English strawberry finally took its lofty seat in the pantheon of fruits.

The strawberry's upward mobility made it a suitable addition to the summertime afternoon teas grazed upon in languorous fashion by people wealthy enough to not be working in the afternoon – a development that coincided with the decision of the All England Croquet and Lawn Tennis Club to hold a tennis tournament at its club ground in Wimbledon in 1877. From the start, afternoon teas replete with strawberries were fundamental to the Wimbledon spectator experience, and the fruit remains inextricably linked with the tournament: for many visitors, a strawberry festival with some tennis in the background. One person who came to regret the fruit's alluring presence at the Championships was six-time winner Blanche Bingley Hillyard, who in 1907 saw her semi-final delayed by rain (another great SW19 tradition) and, thinking play was over, headed to the tea tent to consume, she wrote, a 'fearful meal': 'Two bath buns, six or seven slices of bread and butter, three or four cups of tea, six or seven biscuit cakes, two or three slices of other cake. Not satisfied with that, when I went up to the ladies' dressing-room there were some beautiful strawberries provided for the players, and I ate three plates of these.' Then the rain eased and Hillyard was, despite her vociferous protests, sent back out to play (extremely badly).

Unlike our global reputation for tolerance, stoicism and good humour, Britain's association with the strawberry remains firmly rooted in reality. In fact, our consumption, already considerable, has been on an upward trajectory for several decades. The post-war growth of intensive and highly specialised agriculture and the development of new strawberry varieties and growing systems – particularly the adoption of polytunnels – have improved productivity, made fruit quality even more consistent, and stretched the season far beyond its previous limits. Edward Bunyard wrote of how the strawberry 'receives as warm a welcome in June as does the primrose of spring, and for the same reason,' but today English berries arrive while those primroses are still strongly in bloom. What was once a treat in June and July is now an April to October staple, with demand through the remaining months serviced by shipments from warmer climes. Between 1996 and 2015, consumption of strawberries in the UK soared from sixty-seven thousand tonnes to one hundred and sixty-eight thousand tonnes, the vast majority grown on these islands. The strawberry is now far and away the most valuable British fruit – more valuable, too, than any vegetable crop. In 2017, the entire marketplace for domestically produced fruit was worth £752 million, of which the purchase of strawberries amounted to £283 million – a staggering proportion.

There are now hundreds of strawberry breeds available to growers, varying in colour, flavour, size, firmness, fruiting date and disease resistance, but all of them much plumper and sweeter than those enjoyed by Dr William Butler. Doubtless, God could still make a better berry if he really put his mind to it, but he'd have to work hard to outdo the extraordinary endeavour of the modern horticulturalist.

ALLIUMS

AROUND FOUR THOUSAND YEARS AGO, in the ancient city of Larsa, in what is now Iraq, the world's oldest surviving written recipes were carved into three clay tablets. Currently residing at Yale University, these remarkable artefacts allow us to open a window onto the kitchens of Babylonia and imagine the heady cooking smells that would have billowed from within. One of the tablets, the best preserved, summarises the ingredients for twenty-five stews or broths – twenty-one of them meaty, four of them 'green' – and gives the very briefest of cooking directions, while the other two contain fewer recipes in more detailed form. Between them, what they show is that the Middle East's appetite for spicy lamb stews is absolutely nothing new and that leeks, garlic and onions, the three most common forms of allium, have been fundamental to the creation of such dishes since the dawn of civilisation.

Again and again, these aromatic vegetables are fried in fat at the start of the cooking process; on several occasions, crushed leek and garlic are added again immediately before serving, bringing fresh heat and bite to the finished dish. One fairly typical recipe, for a dish called 'tuh'u', involves searing a leg of mutton, then folding in 'salt, beer, onion, rocket, coriander leaves, Persian shallot, cumin, and red beet . . . leek and garlic'. After sprinkling some coriander seed on top, the cook completes the dish with a little kurrat – another allium, known as Egyptian leek – and a touch more fresh coriander. Despite the vast gulf of time and geography that separates us from ancient Babylonia, it really isn't hard to imagine – and appreciate – how this tagine-like dish would have tasted, and how fundamental to its success the sweet, acidic, umami charms of those alliums would have been.

Domesticated alliums first emerged somewhere in Asia, but where or when is hard to pinpoint. The current concentration of a plant's wild ancestors can often provide a clue to its genesis, but the original precursor to the common onion disappeared long ago, and wild garlic is too abundant to be of any help. Trying to track the progress of alliums through archaeology is similarly futile – their growing and cooking rarely leave much trace – but it is clear from written sources found everywhere from Korea to Egypt that by the time the ancient civilisations of Asia and North Africa began recording their food preferences onto stone, clay, skin and papyrus, these vegetables were firmly established across the world's largest continent and had spilt across large tracts of the continent next door.

It isn't hard to see why. Alliums propagate easily and grow reliably. If carefully processed and stored, some enjoy a rare longevity – when left to cure for a few weeks somewhere cool and shady, the hardiest of onion varieties can last for many months; so too garlic – and the value of any food that can be kept through the winter cannot be overstated. Most importantly, they make everything they touch taste better, either melting deep into the background or bringing a welcome hit of crunch and zip. Wherever alliums were taken they were received with open arms; now, there's barely a corner of the globe where in one form or another they're not considered a native crop.

In Egypt, where their consumption was represented in the decoration of tombs dating back around five thousand years, alliums were among the staple foods of the labourers responsible for the era's greatest feats of engineering: when Herodotus, the ancient Greek historian, visited the pyramid complex of Giza, he was told that sixteen hundred talents of silver, a vast sum of money, was spent on the mountain of radishes, onions and leeks needed to feed the workmen during the construction of the Great Pyramid around 2560 BCE. In Karnak, one of the walls of the temple of Aten, built more than a millennium later, contains a depiction of a worker eating raw onion with bread and cucumber. Alliums were also used by the Egyptians in funerary rites: onions could be used to fill the body's cavities (for the mummy of Ramses IV, they served as false eyes), and preserved bulbs of garlic were found among the more gilded treasures of Tutankhamun's tomb. These vegetables clearly had a symbolic power – Pliny the Elder mentioned them being 'invoked by the Egyptians when taking an oath' – but the Roman poet Juvenal, a man with a colourful imagination and a track-record of writing statements about Egypt that probably weren't true, may have overstated things slightly when he suggested that alliums were worshipped as gods: 'It is an impious outrage to crunch leeks and onions with the teeth / What a holy race to have such divinities springing up in their gardens!'

According to the Bible, it was while in captivity in Egypt that the Jews first developed a taste for alliums. In the Book of Numbers, the absence of delicious vegetables became a major source of irritation among the hungry, weary Israelites as they made their slow walk through the mountains and deserts towards the Promised Land. 'We remember the fish which we did eat in Egypt freely: the cucumbers and the melons, and the leeks, and the onions, and the garlic,' they lamented. 'But now our soul is dried away, there is nothing at all, besides this manna, before our eyes.' And while the entire story of the Jews' captivity and exodus is historically questionable, the enduring centrality of onions and garlic to Jewish culinary culture is absolutely not.

In *The Natural History*, Pliny provided an exhaustive list of the various onion varieties enjoyed in ancient Roman society, including the tiny, sweet Setanian onion, the Schistan onion, which could be stored through the winter with its leaves still on, and one from Cyprus, which, more than any other, 'draws tears from the eyes'. He described the 'peculiar nature' of the Ascalonian onion – probably a shallot – and wrote of how the spring onion was 'employed for seasonings'. He also told the entertaining tale of how the leek (the most prized of which came from Egypt) had 'recently acquired considerable celebrity from the use made of it by the Emperor Nero. That prince, to improve his voice, used to eat leeks and oil every month, upon stated days, abstaining from every other kind of food, and not touching so much as a morsel of bread even'. Pliny didn't say how effective this was, but if leeks do improve singing that would certainly explain the Welsh.

* * *

Throughout history, the one member of the almost universally loved allium family that has proved consistently divisive has been garlic, enjoyed by many for the complex, musky flavours it imparts but derided by others for its pungency and stench. In his *Epodes* (c.30 BCE), the Roman poet Horace howled with righteous disgust after being served a garlicky dinner: 'If any man, with impious hand, should ever / Strangle an aged parent, / Make him eat garlic, it's deadlier than hemlock, / O you strong stomachs that cull it! / What poison is this that's burning my entrails? / Has viper's blood mixed with these herbs / Betrayed me?' The punishment Horace wished upon the garlic-loving friend who had fed him the dish was that 'your girl with her hands obstructs your kisses, / And takes the far side of the bed!'

This – the passion-killing effect of alliaceous breath – was a consistent source of humour in the ancient world (as one Martial epigram advised, 'Whenever you have eaten strong-smelling shreds of the Tarentine leek, give kisses with your mouth shut'). Perhaps unfairly, then, alliums were also widely believed to boost male virility. In the Talmud, a set of laws attributed to the great scribe Ezra, Jewish men were instructed to eat garlic the night before the Sabbath, to help them make the most of the holiday, while in Rome, onions were seen as a reliable source of potency – unless, according to Martial, 'your wife is old, and your member languid,' in which case 'bulbs can do no more for you than fill your belly'.

The Perfumed Garden, a glorious work of fifteenth-century Arabic smut, abounded with men who, stuffed to the gunnels with onions, embarked on erotic adventures that would prove eye-watering in every sense. One verse began: 'The member of Abou el Heiloukh has remained erect / For thirty days without a break, because he did eat onions.' The text also offered an intriguingly multi-stage recipe for increasing masculine endowment: procure an ass's penis and boil it, together with onions and a large quantity of corn, then 'with this dish feed fowls, which you eat afterwards'. In somewhat less explicit terms, Geoffrey Chaucer's *The Canterbury Tales* (c.1400) made a nod towards that same quality. In the book's Prologue, the summoner, a red-faced, lecherous church official, had his dietary preferences clearly outlined: 'Wel loved he garleek, oynons, and eek lekes, / And for to drynken strong wyn, reed as blood.' Readers would have had no doubt at all about the proclivities of such a prolific eater of alliums. Even leeks, among the mildest of alliums, had power enough. 'The Welch, who eat them much,' wrote the seventeenth-century writer and gardener John Evelyn, 'are observ'd to be very fruitful'.

This belief in the amorous nature of alliums reflected their place in the complex matrix of Galenic medicine. Onions, leeks and garlic were, like cinnamon, considered hot and dry, so their consumption would heat the bodily humours – good for a bit of hot-blooded action, bad if you happened to be, in Galen's words, 'bilious in nature'. While everyone, wrote Galen in the second century, should be 'sparing in the regular consumption' of these vegetables, their nature could have medical benefits for 'those who have accumulated mucus or crude, thick, viscid humours'. If your health and character were being affected by an undue thickness of blood, phlegm or black bile, garlic – the hottest and driest of alliums – should be eaten as a 'health-giving medication, since it has the ability to remove and disperse obstructions'.

This ancient faith in the medical power of alliums persisted across Europe and the Islamic world and proved particularly compelling here in Britain where the cold, wet climate meant that the fight against thick phlegm remained a constant one. In sixteenth-century England, John Gerard wrote that garlic was commonly known as 'poore men's treacle' (back then, treacle, a word derived from the Latin *theriaca*, was a name given to any powerful remedy). As well as noting its ability to cut through bodily humours that are 'tough and clammie', Gerard considered garlic to be an 'enimie to all colde poisons, and to the bitings of venemous beasts'. Onion, too, had benefits: it was 'good against the biting of a mad dogge' (vaguely plausible given the antiseptic quality of onion juice) and 'annointed upon a . . . balde head in the sunne, bringeth againe the haire very speedily,' (less plausible, but worth a try). Leeks also worked their warm, dry magic: John Parkinson, a contemporary of Gerard, described their ability to 'free the chest and lungs from much corruption,' and that the green leaves, 'being boyled and applyed warme to the hemorrhoides or piles, when they are swolne and painfull, give a great deale of ease'.

After domesticated alliums were brought to Britain by the Romans, they became a staple food of ploughmen and kings alike. In the fourteenth-century poem *Piers Plowman* they were included among the meagre foods with which 'the poor people' attempted to 'please Hunger', while that same century they also appeared on page after page of

Richard II's royal cookbook *The Forme of Cury* (c.1390). John Parkinson attempted to summarise their various uses in the country's kitchens before rather lamely giving up, so onerous did the task prove: 'Onions are used many wayes, as sliced and put into pottage, or boyled and peeled and layde in dishes for sallets at supper, or sliced and put into water, for a sawce for mutton or oysters, or into meate roasted being stuffed with parsly, and so many waies that I cannot recount them, every one pleasing themselves, according to their order, manner or delight.'

In nineteenth-century London, the poor continued to please Hunger with onions. In *Oliver Twist* (1838), Charles Dickens painted a vivid picture of a workhouse where, having been given the choice of 'being starved by a gradual process in the house, or by a quick one out of it,' residents were served 'three meals of thin gruel a day, with an onion twice a week, and half a roll of Sundays'. In *London Labour and the London Poor* (1861), the journalist Henry Mayhew reported: 'The greatest sum of money expended by the poor upon any vegetable (after potatoes) is spent upon onions . . . To those who know the habits of the poor, this will appear in no way singular, a piece of bread and an onion being to the English labourer what bread and an apple or a bunch of grapes is to the French peasant – often his dinner.' The same year Mayhew's book was published, Mrs Beeton, whose recipe collection essayed the diet of those who either were or aspired to be well-to-do, described how respectable households retained a similar penchant for whole onions: 'With many, the onion is a very great favourite . . . The Spanish kind is frequently taken for supper, it being simply boiled, and then seasoned with salt, pepper, and butter. Some dredge on a little flour, but many prefer it without this.'

According to Mayhew, the fancy Iberian varieties – milder and sweeter than their English cousins – were sold by young Jewish traders who had cornered the market for 'Bahama pineapples and of the Spanish and Portuguese onions'. The cheap, pungent native onions eaten by the poor were peddled mainly by Irish women, who fashioned them into 'ropes': bunches of between six and forty-eight bulbs, their roots skilfully plaited together with a length of straw. Around a thousand of these traders worked the London streets, drawn by the low barriers to entry. 'Onion selling can be started on a small amount of capital, from 6d to 1s, which is no doubt one inducement for those poor persons to resort to it,' Mayhew explained. He also presented a vivid scene of a Saturday night street market in which 'little boys, holding three or four onions in their hand, creep between the people, wriggling their way through every interstice, and asking for custom in whining tones, as if seeking charity'.

Notably, though, Mayhew made no mention at all of traders selling garlic. According to Mrs Beeton, who avoided it as best she could, 'the smell of this plant is generally considered offensive, and it is the most acrimonious in its taste of the whole of the alliaceous tribe'. She also noted that garlic 'was in greater repute with our ancestors than it is with ourselves,' a reflection perhaps of the fading belief in its medicinal properties. There's a Garlick Hill in London and a Garlic Row in Cambridge, both at the sites of medieval markets, suggesting that once it was sold in sizeable quantities, and it appeared with some regularity in the very earliest English cookbooks – in *The Forme of Cury*, it cropped up in sauces for chicken, goose, pigeon and conger eel, and was one of the essential ingredients in a 'salat', alongside leeks, onions, fennel and a host of soft herbs. Three hundred years later, though, in his *Acetaria: A Discourse Of Sallets* (1699), John Evelyn stated of garlic that the British 'absolutely forbid it entrance into our salleting, by reason of its intolerable rankness'. As far as he was concerned, the only people who should eat it were 'northern rustics', especially those who live in 'moist places', or possibly sailors, but 'to be sure, 'tis not for ladies' palats, nor those who court them'. He also stated that 'the eating of it was (as we read) part of the punishment for such as had committed the horrid'st crimes' – a claim lacking any evidence, but one that would surely have been applauded by our Roman friend Horace.

Evelyn noted that garlic was 'both by Spaniards and Italians, and the more southern people, familiarly eaten, with almost everything,' and the British mistrust of garlic was widely tied to a racist association with dirty, effete southern Europeans. In a letter sent from Naples in 1818, the poet Percy Shelley informed a friend that Italian count-esses 'smell so of garlick that an ordinary Englishman cannot approach them' – although, as he pointed out, even that didn't stop Lord Byron. Garlic's musky charms did eventu-ally find favour among wealthy, well-travelled types who liked to flaunt their cosmopolitan tastes, but most people were having none of it. In 1944, George Orwell wrote that the British working class 'regard such things as garlic and olive oil with disgust,' demanding instead 'tea and puddings'. Really, it's only in the past thirty years or so that garlic has become a staple of the British kitchen rather than just a staple of jokes about French people's breath.

Had there been a crisis in the supply of garlic during the Second World War, it's unlikely that Britons would have cared – or even noticed. But the crisis came in the onion supply, and that really was a problem. For decades, even as the nation's consumption of onions had been steadily rising, the amount of land given over to their production was in decline. With its European trade networks and a global empire whose resources could be exploited to fill British bellies, the UK had reached a position where it no longer felt obliged to grow its own food, and farmers were instead able to concentrate on whatever crops were most lucrative. In 1936, *The Times* newspaper reported that 'severe foreign competition has made it unprofitable to grow a crop which occupies the ground so long and involves such a high expenditure on hand labour'.

As British farms were turned over to faster-growing, higher-margin produce, onions poured in from Spain, France, the Netherlands and as far away as Bermuda, a British colony famous for its onion crop. ('The onion is the pride and joy of Bermuda,' wrote Mark Twain in 1877 after visiting the island. 'It is her jewel, her gem of gems.') One very visible source was the region of Roscoff in Brittany, home to a pink-skinned variety much admired for its flavour. In the early twentieth century, Breton onion merchants began sailing to England to hawk their wares door to door. Their numbers peaked in 1929 when around fourteen hundred sellers made the trip, many of them bringing with them bicycles to speed up their rounds. The popular British stereotype of the Frenchman wearing a beret and striped shirt and riding a bike swaddled in onions was born of these Onion Johnnies being the only representatives of their country that most people on this side of the Channel ever met. It's a stereotype of such strange specificity that the French are for the most part baffled by it.

When the war broke out in 1939, just about every onion consumed in the UK was being shipped from abroad. As borders quickly closed, the supply disappeared almost overnight. A government poster campaign to encourage planting did little to help, and as availability shrank, prices swelled. In February 1941, the staff at *The Times* raffled a large onion for over £4 – more than the average weekly wage – and in 1943, one American visitor described this unlikely scene: 'Served as a side dish at our luncheon of the regular three-course meal, which Englishmen religiously impose upon themselves in conformity with ration regulations, was a medium-size boiled Spanish onion. "You've been robbing a bank or playing with the black market," exclaimed the astonished husband.'

After the war, the onion supply gradually returned to normal, and the British could once again give proper depth to their shepherd's pies and Lancashire hotpots, but the underlying problem has never really been fixed. Despite its rich and plentiful agricultural land, the UK remains a country that expects the rest of the world to provide it with fresh produce while its own food industry focuses on growing animal feed and manufacturing alcohol and heavily processed foods. In 2018, well over half of the onions bought in Britain were shipped from overseas. In total, just under seventy per cent of the money we spent on vegetables went on imports, and the imbalance for fruit was even more extreme. We also have very little by way of a plan to deal with whatever shocks to the system await, and those shocks have, of late, been coming thick and fast. The message is clear: start planting or start saving up – those onion raffles could soon be coming back.

EEL

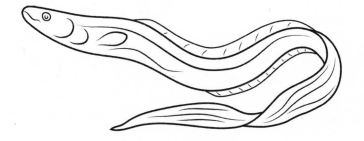

I N THE SPRING AND SUMMER of 1877, a desperate call for public assistance was printed in newspapers all across Germany. 'In spite of all our modern aids, science has not yet succeeded in clearing up the mystery of the propagation of the eel,' the notice stated. 'The German Fishery Association at Berlin will, therefore, pay a reward of fifty marks to anyone who will send . . . an eel in a state of pregnancy sufficiently advanced to throw some light on the [mystery].'

This unusual request (and its generous monetary reward) certainly struck a chord. Fisheries staff were at first delighted, then increasingly appalled, by the scale of the response. Overwhelmed by deliveries of rotting fish detritus, the Royal Superintendent of Fisheries was compelled to publish a follow-up asking that people only send in whole eels, rather than packing up and posting off what were claimed to be baby eels but were clearly the parasitic contents of their dinner's digestive systems. 'Most of the senders have sent me only the intestines, or also the supposed young of the eel, which invariably turned out to be intestinal worms,' he complained. '[They] have eaten the eel, and nevertheless requested to have the fifty marks forwarded to them, often by return mail.'

That researchers in one of the world's most scientifically advanced countries had resorted to such an ill-conceived crowd-sourcing campaign in the futile pursuit of a pregnant eel is an indication of just how much this most obtuse of fish had messed with their heads – and they were far from the first to be tormented by its inscrutable nature. On the surface, the European freshwater eel is among the dreariest of God's creations: a tube with eyes; a squirming, expressionless hose of slimy skin and fatty flesh. And yet nothing could be further from the truth. The eel, far from being dull, is one of nature's great enigmas: a riddle, wrapped in a mystery, wrapped (in London's few remaining pie and mash shops) in jelly.

As Sir Humphry Davy, one of the greatest scientists of the nineteenth century, put it: 'The problem of their generation is the most abstruse, and one of the most curious in natural history.' At the heart of this problem was the eel's ability to exist in large quantities across Europe without ever appearing to breed. Where to find them, how to land them, how to cook them: all that was common knowledge – but where they came from muddled even the finest of minds. Aristotle, whose synthesis of science, logic, ethics and linguistics would shape the lexicon of western intellectual enquiry, made some typically acute observations of the eel's behaviour in his *History of Animals*, but his analysis of how they reproduce was, quite frankly, rubbish. Eels, he wrote, are 'derived' from the 'earth's guts', emerging from 'earthworms' that 'grow spontaneously in mud and in humid ground . . . both in the sea and in rivers, especially where there is decayed matter: in the sea in places where sea-weed abounds, and in rivers and marshes near to the edge; for it is near to the water's edge that sun-heat has its chief power and produces putrefaction.' In ancient Rome, Pliny the Elder hardly covered himself in glory by surmising that eels 'rub themselves against rocks, upon which the particles they thus scrape from their bodies come to life'. Oppian, a second-century Greco-Roman poet who at least had the excuse of not being a scientist, believed that when closely entwined, the fish 'writhe their moist bodies, and from them a fluid-like foam flows and is covered by the sands; and the mud receives it and conceives, and gives birth to the trailing eel'.

Centuries later, the confusion continued. The seventeenth-century writer Izaak Walton provided a typically lyrical summary of some of his era's competing theories: 'And others say, that eels, growing old, breed other eels out of the corruption of their own age . . . And others say, that as pearls are made of glutinous dewdrops, which are condensed by the sun's heat in those countries, so eels are bred of a particular dew, falling in the months of May or June on the banks of some particular ponds or rivers, apted by nature for that end; which in a few days are, by the sun's heat, turned into eels.'

One common theory was that eels are viviparous, meaning their young are not hatched from eggs like most other fish (sharks being the major exception) but are born fully formed, like mammals. Even the great Carl Linnaeus, a giant of eighteenth-century natural sciences, wrongly supposed that eels give birth to live young. But Aristotle, despite letting himself down with the whole 'spontaneously generated earthworms' hypothesis, applied a higher standard of reason when dismissing the belief that young eels grew from 'hair-like' progeny found within the stomachs of sliced-open adults. 'Animals that are viviparous have their young in the womb and closely attached, and not in the belly; for, if the embryo were kept in the belly, it would be subjected to the process of digestion, like ordinary food,' he wrote. As the German Fishery Association's scientists would attest after assessing their putrid haul of parasitic worms, those hair-like progeny are definitely not baby eels.

And yet, what we now know to be true of the eel's lifecycle is really no less outrageous than any of history's wilder hypotheses. The reason that no one had ever seen European eels mating, laying eggs or hatching is that no European eel has ever mated, laid eggs or hatched anywhere near Europe. Instead, they all, without exception, appear to do so in the warm blue waters of the Sargasso Sea, near the Bahamas. From there, billions of larval eels (*Leptocephalus*) – tiny, ghostly, sinister-looking filaments of transparent flesh – are propelled thousands of miles across the vast ocean. By the time these migrants, nicknamed 'thin-heads', arrive on our side of the Atlantic, they have morphed into glass eels – still tiny and transparent but more obviously eel-like and less nightmarish. As they dart into estuaries and make contact with fresh water, they pause for their respiratory systems to adapt, before – now known colloquially as elvers – forging upriver, leaving the water if necessary to scale dams or clamber over rocks and vegetation (As Oppian wrote, eels number 'among the stern sea-monsters which leave the salt water and come forth upon the life-giving soil of the dry land'). In the rivers and lakes, they hide in mud during the day, then feed voraciously at night on whatever they can find, including fish, other eels, ducks (according to one Victorian book editor at least) and, if some accounts are to be believed, garden vegetables – the thirteenth-century German theologian Albertus Magnus wrote of how the eel 'is said sometimes by night to crawl out of the water on the fields where it finds lentils, peas and beans'.

For anything between eight and forty years, the eel will grow longer and fatter, some becoming vast in scale (a Scottish loch was described in the eighteenth century as having eels 'as bigg as ane horse'; so big that only one 'ancient fisher' in the entire region owned a rod strong enough to land them). As it fattens, it changes in colour from glassy to yellow-brown to silver. Then, one dark, stormy autumnal night, when the moon is in its last quarter, a switch deep within is suddenly flicked, causing it to charge back downriver towards the sea. In a surge of slick, writhing flesh, mature eels come pouring en masse out of the estuaries, adapting once more to salinity, then finding their way – somehow – back across epic reaches of the Atlantic, all the way to the Caribbean. In the Sargasso Sea, their sex organs having developed along the way, they mate for the first and only time. And then they die.

Even now, in an era of particle colliders and monkey cloning, significant gaps remain in our understanding of this process. It is unsurprising, then, that unravelling the eel's mysteries took so long. In the eighteenth century, several Italian scientists, including the pioneering anatomist Carlo Mondini, produced increasingly convincing evidence that a frill-like band attached to the swim bladder of some larger eels was in fact an immature ovary. The hunt was then on to find an eel with testicles. In 1876, as a graduate research student at Vienna University, Sigmund Freud was sent to a laboratory in Trieste to help test the claim by Polish zoologist Szymon Syrski that a set of tiny lobes observed in an eel were its gonads. After painstakingly dissecting and microscopically examining hundreds of specimens, Freud's conclusions, published the following year, were inconclusive at best. After dabbling with the riddle of eel testicles, Freud's subsequent career path – attempting to unravel the byzantine mysteries of human psychology and sexuality – would prove far less problematic. Syrski did, though, seem to be onto something and by the end of the nineteenth century it was generally agreed that eels are not, as Aristotle had claimed, 'neither male nor female'; that instead they are, like most fish, oviparous (egg layers); that males are smaller than females; and that when they spawn, they do so not in Europe's rivers and lakes but somewhere far out to sea.

The eventual discovery of that 'somewhere' was down to Johannes Schmidt – a slightly slapdash, unnecessarily chippy, but deeply visionary Danish researcher. Building on (while loudly belittling) the work of Giovanni Battista Grassi, an Italian who in 1896 had produced the first proof that *Leptocephalus* – previously thought to be a distinct species – was the larval form of the eel, Schmidt spent years logging the length of any thin-heads he managed to pluck from the seas around Europe and incorporating data from the more substantial catches of rival marine biologists. The further south and west the catch, the smaller the thin-heads contained within it – so south and west he went, out into the Atlantic. In 1920, seven years after a first ocean-going mission had ended with an expensive shipwreck and a nagging but unproven belief that the Sargasso Sea might be the source, the Dane set off once more to test his theory, and this time managed to haul in a catch of thin-heads much smaller than any recorded before. He returned to the target site at the start of the following year and in April 1921 caught an abundance of thin-heads so tiny that they must have hatched right there just days before. The most abstruse and curious mystery in natural history had finally been solved.

The bizarre lifecycle of the eel shaped Europe's relationship to it as a foodstuff. The annual arrival of glass eels presented a short glut of small, wormlike fish that could be caught in fine-meshed nets and then fried like whitebait. There are some parts of the continent – most notably the Basque Country – that have an abiding appetite for glass eels, but very little interest in eating mature adults. A wave of elvers reached England's rivers in the springtime – the Severn, in particular, was once famous for the vast scale of this fishy ingress, while one account from 1600 described the Avon 'covered over and coloured black with little eels scarce so big as a goose quill,' which locals would 'scoop up in great numbers'. Izaak Walton wrote of a pond in Staffordshire 'where, about a set time in summer, such small eels abound so much, that many of the poorer sort of people that inhabit near to it, take such eels out of this mere with sieves or sheets; and make a kind of eel-cake of them, and eat it like as bread'. In 1533, out of concern for adult eel stocks, Henry VIII outlawed the taking of 'any frye, spaune or brode of yeles called yele fares or ell vares,' and the work of the English elverman has across the centuries frequently been either banned or (as is the case now) highly restricted.

While the arrival of glass eels and elvers was eagerly anticipated, the autumnal rush of big, fat eels back towards the sea produced an even more valuable catch, staggering in its size and quality. Pliny the Elder wrote of how Italian fishermen would set traps at the point where Lake Garda discharges into the Mincio River: 'At the part of it whence this river issues, once a year, and mostly in the month of October, the lake is troubled, evidently by the constellations of autumn, and the eels are heaped together by the waves, and rolled on by them in such astonishing multitudes, that single masses of them, containing more than a thousand in number, are often taken in the chambers which are formed in the bed of the river for that purpose.' More than eighteen hundred years later, another Italian writer, Pellegrino Artusi, described the same autumnal ritual – known locally as *la calata* ('the descent') – in the Valli di Comacchio of Emilia-Romagna, insisting that 'on a single dark, stormy night in October 1905, one hundred and fifty thousand kilos of eels were caught,' landed using equipment of no greater sophistication than was used in Pliny's time.

While autumn was prime time for eel eaters, Europeans enjoyed the abundant presence of these sweet-fleshed, energy-rich fish in the continent's river and lakes all year round. Sedentary in the daytime, landing them required nothing more than a spear or a primitive trap, making them a food source ripe for exploitation by even the most primitive of societies. According to Oppian, some youths 'in havens of the sea beyond the wash of the waves,' would, just for the kicks, fish for eels using nothing but a length of sheep gut, dangled in the water. When an eel latched on to the intestine, the young fisherman would inflate it like a balloon by blowing as hard as possible on the other end: 'By his vehement blowing the gut swells up and fills the straining mouth of wretched eel; which is straitened and distressed by the human breath, but is held a fast prisoner for all its endeavour to escape, until, swollen and wildly gasping, it swims to the surface and becomes the prey of the fisher.'

In ancient Greece, eels were a delicacy, served up at weddings and feasts. 'I do think in short that of all fish the best in flavour is the noble eel,' stated the poet Archestratus, who considered those caught along the strait between Sicily and Calabria to be the best. In common with many Hellenic writers, he also reserved praise for the 'large and wonderfully fat' eels found in Lake Copais, in Boeotia, central Greece. Athenaeus, whose *Deipnosophistae*, a vast collection of food writing compiled in the second century BCE, abounded with references to the culinary charms of the eel, perhaps best summed up the Greek attitude to eels by quoting from a poem by Philetærus accusing rich men who live sparingly of being the 'most truly miserable': 'For when you're dead, you cannot then eat eels; / No wedding feasts are cook'd in Pluto's realms.'

Greeks may have loved eating eels, but Egyptians took their veneration a step further. Considered one of the incarnations of the god Atum, they were treated with reverence in life and in death – the British Museum displays a particularly fine bronze container for an eel mummy, dating from the Ptolemaic era. Herodotus, the fifth-century BCE Greek historian who wrote extensively about Egypt, claimed that eels, otters, scale-fish and the fox-goose were 'said to be sacred to the god of the Nile'. His countrymen found this all quite amusing, with plenty of Greek writers poking fun at the Egyptians for their choice of idol. As Anaxandrides put it: 'You do think / An eel the mightiest of deities; / But we do eat him as the best of fish.' Antiphanes joked that Egyptians were right to treat eels as deities, though, given how much they cost. The Olympian gods, he wrote, 'we gain over by our prayers alone; / But as for eels, without you spend at least / Twelve drachmas you can scarce get leave to smell them'.

In ancient Rome, there was a touch more ambivalence. Juvenal called the eel 'an unwholesome breed which fattens where Cloaca's torrents pour,' while the *De Re Coquinaria* cookbook included very few eel recipes, but one, quite pointedly, for a sauce by which eel 'will be made more palatable,' containing a load of quite forceful ingredients, including pepper, anise, sumac and mustard. Subsequently, though, Italians proved deeply appreciative of the fish, which became a Christmas Eve staple. Eels taken from the Valli di Comacchio were praised by the most famous chef of the Italian Renaissance, Bartolomeo Scappi, as being the 'best of any place in Lombardy,' salted specimens of which were 'carried throughout Italy'. The finest eels available in Rome came, he said, from Lake Bolsena in central Italy, and these also appeared in Dante's *Divine Comedy* (c.1320) in an allusion to the reviled Pope Martin IV, whose appetite for pickled Bolsena eels supposedly led to his death by choking.

The English have always loved an eel, be it baked, roasted, boiled, stewed, soused, spatchcocked or, as with every other ingredient these tribes have yet encountered, baked into a pie. The Venerable Bede, in his *Ecclesiastical History of the*

English People (c.731), described this as a land with 'the greatest plenty' of eels – so plentiful, he suggested, that the ignorant pagan Saxons of the south-east for years fished only for eels until taught about both God and sea fishing by Bishop Wilfrid, an enlightened northerner. Bede also mentioned that Ely, in the East Anglian fens, 'has its name from the great plenty of eels taken in those marshes'. For several centuries, eels were sufficiently plentiful and economically valuable to be used as a medium of exchange. As early as the seventh century, the rents charged by Ine, the Saxon king of Wessex, included hundreds of eels. Around three hundred years later, the *Ely Farming Memoranda* described a fen being rented from Ely Abbey at a cost of 26,275 eels, and the *Domesday Book*, collated in 1086, contained dozens of entries for eels being used to pay rents to abbeys and manors – these were dotted all over the country, but particularly clustered in East Anglia, and were measured in 'sticks', with each stick consisting of twenty-five fish.

In William Shakespeare's *King Lear*, the Fool makes mocking reference to a foolish 'cockney' trying to make an eel pie. And while people all over the country have traditionally eaten eels in vast quantities, it is cockneys who are most closely associated with the fish in the modern imagination. In 1854, the doctor and essayist David Badham described London as a city filled with street traders hawking vast quantities of stewed eel to the working classes and 'some of the inferior bourgeoisie': 'London, from one end to the other, teems and steams with eels, alive and stewed; turn where you will, "hot eels" are everywhere smoking away, with many a fragrant condiment at hand to make what is in itself palatable yet more savoury; and this too at so low a rate, that for one halfpenny a man . . . may fill his stomach with six or seven long pieces, and wash them down with a cupful of the glutinous liquor in which they have been stewed.' When left to cool, this liquor would, thanks to the fish's gelatinous proteins, form a flavoursome jelly, and cold chunks of jellied eel became one of London's defining dishes, to the screaming horror of almost every other food culture.

One of the most remarkable things about London's vast eel habit was where the fish came from. The Thames had once abounded with eels, but as the city grew (and demand for eels grew with it), so too did the quantity of ordure pouring into the river. Eels, as had long been understood, do not cope well with filth (Aristotle wrote of their love of 'perfectly clear' water), so alternative sources had to be found. Dutch ships, which began supplying eels to London as early as the fifteenth century, became sufficiently indispensable that when a law was passed in 1699 'for the better encouragement of the fishery of this kingdom,' making it illegal for foreign fishermen to sell their catch in England, live eels were one of only two exceptions (the other being dried cod). These imports weren't always held in high regard – 'the Thames silver eel is generally esteemed the best, and the worst are brought by the Dutch and sold at Billingsgate; there is a greater difference in the goodness of eels than in any other fish,' sniffed Richard Dolby in *The Cook's Dictionary* (1830) – but by midway through the nineteenth century, the Netherlands had a virtual monopoly on the London trade. In 1861, of the eight hundred and fifty tonnes of eel sold at Billingsgate Market, eight hundred tonnes were Dutch. Their vessels, known as *schuyts* (a name that sounds not unlike one of the major Thames pollutants), had large water tanks built into their holds, in which eels could be kept alive for weeks, allowing the Dutch to carry them here from all around northern Europe. Eventually, the Thames became so polluted that the schuyts could no longer moor anywhere close to Billingsgate without their precious cargo dying almost instantly. The boats were forced further and further out: first Erith, then Gravesend, then Holehaven Creek.

The Thames is now clean enough to support eels once again. Tragically, though, there aren't nearly enough eels in existence for many of them to find their way here. In the past few decades, the European eel population has collapsed, with the number of glass eels arriving each year falling by as much as ninety-five per cent since 1980. Where once the mystery was where eels came from, the mystery now is where they've all gone. The effects of climate change on the strength and direction of the Gulf Stream – essential, it seems, to the journey of the larval eels – are likely to be a major factor. So too pollution in the Sargasso Sea. Overfishing by Europeans, particularly of glass eels (including large-scale illegal trafficking of glass eels to Asia), is also a major problem. With most fish species native to Europe, it is possible to regulate catches in a way that protects their reproductive cycles, but because eels spawn just once, many thousands of miles away, every single one that is plucked from our waters, whether a glass eel or a fully grown adult, is a fish that will never have the chance to mate. There are some fish-eries in Europe that, by catching young eels and farming only a small proportion to maturity while transporting the rest across various hazards to live wild in their natural habits, make a solid claim to be aiding the sustainability of the world's stocks, but in truth, it is very hard for anyone today to eat eel without asking searching questions about the ethics of doing so.

Throughout the long history of these islands, it would have seemed inconceivable that a food market like Borough, located just metres from Britain's largest river, would not abound with eels, living or preserved, but that is the sad situation we find ourselves in. Less than a century after finally uncovering the truth about its lifecycle, this dull-looking but utterly extraordinary tube with eyes may be on the verge of disappearing forever.

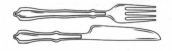

ICE CREAM

N OT ALL THE TIPS OFFERED up to wine drinkers by the Neapolitan academic Giambattista della Porta in *Natural Magick*, his 1589 masterpiece of natural philosophy, proved particularly effective. His instruction that alcoholism could be cured by drowning three live eels in a barrel of wine and then drinking the liquor was probably best ignored. So too his insistence that 'the filth of a dog's ear, mingled with wine' offered a shortcut to drunkenness (although it would mirror the flavour profile of mass-market chardonnay).

But his instructions for chilling wine were built on far sounder foundations. 'The chief thing desired at feasts is that wine cold as ice may be drunk, especially in summer,' he explained, not unreasonably. 'I will teach you how wine shall presently not only grow cold, but freezes that you cannot drink it but by sucking, and drawing in of your breath.' To achieve this magical effect, the party people of Naples were advised to 'put wine into a vial, and put a little water to it, that it may turn to ice the sooner, then cast snow into a wooden vessel, and strew into it saltpetre, powdered . . . Turn the vial in the snow, and ice will congeal by degrees'. And unlikely though that may sound, it worked.

What della Porta was describing was a surprisingly simple chemical reaction, the gradual proliferation of which brought an extra thrill to wine-drenched festivities on hot Campania nights and set in motion the gradual evolution of the ice cream. Saltpetre, the mineral form of potassium nitrate, crystals of which are found encrusted on cave walls, is an essential component in the production of gunpowder – but it can also be used for a more benign function. For reasons far too complex to explore in detail, when saltpetre is mixed with ice the freezing point of this icy blend plummets below zero, causing it to both melt and – seemingly perversely – get colder. If a vessel containing another liquid – be that water, della Porta's wine or some sweetened milk and cream – is plunged into the super-cooled slush, then slowly shaken and turned, the liquid contents of that vessel will begin to freeze.

Like so many medieval innovations, knowledge of this process made its way to Europe from the more scientifically advanced civilisations of the east: the earliest surviving written reference to the use of saltpetre in the creation of ice dated from around 1245 in a book by the Syrian Arab physician Ibn Abi Usaibia, who made no claim to the invention, having read about it in an earlier (and now seemingly lost) work. It appears that the Mughal emperors – the central Asian dynasty that took control of most of the Indian subcontinent from the early sixteenth century – became enthusiastic adopters of the technique: frozen drinks were described as a 'source of joy for great and small' at the court of Emperor Akbar.

That Italy was the European testbed for this science should come as no great surprise. It was Italian city-states, particularly Venice and Genoa, that became the primary conduits of trade with the east, and ideas flowed along these well-established trade routes with much the same ease as goods. The making of ices was first alluded to in 1530 by Marcantonio Zimara, a philosopher at Padua University, in a treatise on the works of Aristotle. Twenty years later, the Spanish physician Blas Villafranca, who lived in Rome, instructed his readers to harness saltpetre in the pursuit of refreshment, while declaring that frozen drinks were becoming all the rage in Roman high society (probably an exaggeration, given that nobody who wasn't a doctor would mention the phenomenon until several decades later). From Italy, the knowledge flowed onwards, and began to appear in the writings of academics in other parts of Europe – in 1559, the use of saltpetre was mentioned by Dutch physician Levinus Lemnius as a method by which 'wine in cask may not soon grow sowre'.

Initially, as all these early references make clear, the drink to which the method was most widely applied was wine (which needed to be heavily diluted for the chemistry to work), but other popular drinks were also ripe for being jazzed up with natural magic. Foremost among these was another invention recently appropriated from Asia: the sherbet, a complex blend of fruit juices, flower waters and sugar enjoyed across the Islamic world, where the consumption of alcohol was forbidden. Central to a well-constructed sherbet's appeal was its ability to take the heat out of a sweltering summer's day, but this quality only came to the fore if the drink had been properly chilled (using conventional ice cubes rather than minerals scraped from cave walls). As Pierre Belon, a Frenchman who travelled to the

Middle East in the late 1540s, wrote: 'Some are made of figs, others of plums, and of pears and peaches, others again of apricots and grapes, yet others of honey, and the sherbet-maker mixes snow or ice with them, to cool them: for otherwise there would be no pleasure in drinking them.'

These cold, fragrant, syrupy beverages found favour in Italy, a land of hot weather and stunning fruit, and the drinking of sherbets became fashionable among Italians of wealth and status who enjoyed their exotic allure and had access to properly insulated ice houses. In 1577, Francesco, the Grand Duke of Tuscany and patriarch of the wealthy Medici family, wrote to Mafeo Veniero, a Venetian aristocrat, asking that he send him a sherbet recipe – an endorsement from the very highest echelon of society. (The duke, incidentally, was a big fan of cold drinks – he was reported by one contemporary to have habitually drunk a mixture of white grape must and iced milk 'at strange hours'.) As these drinks became increasingly popular in the century that followed, thanks in part to a burgeoning trade in pre-mixed sherbet powders and solids from the Levant, which made them accessible to people who had no access to essential oils, musk, ambergris and sugar, the overheated population of southern Italy began experimenting with della Porta's chemistry in the pursuit of fruit drinks that were not just chilled but frozen. This was made much simpler – and, crucially, cheaper – after about 1620, as the realisation dawned (as first described by the English scientist Francis Bacon) that common salt worked just as well as saltpetre in the supercooling of ice, while also being far more likely to be found in the average pantry. Once it became apparent that sherbets – *sorbette* in Italian – would, as long as sufficient sugar had been added to them, freeze with a pleasing texture (much more so than wine), these icy treats became a fixture of Italian cuisine, particularly in Naples.

In 1692, Antonio Latini, who had moved to Naples to become steward to a senior politician in the Spanish regime that governed the region, made reference to his adopted city's culinary obsession: 'In the city of Naples a great quantity of "sorbette" are consumed, and they are the consistency of sugar and snow, and every Neapolitan, it would seem, is born with the knowledge of how to make them.' Latini may not have been born with the knowledge, but he clearly learnt it. In his book, *Lo Scalco alla Moderna*, he offered several recipes for ices, including one for 'sorbetta di limone', two made with chocolate – one frozen solid in bricks, the other a mousse stirred as it froze (notably, his only mention of stirring, a process vital to the creation of a smooth ice) – and others flavoured with cinnamon, strawberry and cherry. As well as water ices, dairy-based liquids were also being plunged into the salty slush: Latini described a 'sorbetta di latte', made from milk, water, sugar and either candied citron or *cocuzzata*, a type of squash – not nearly creamy enough to count as an ice cream, but certainly a step along that road.

It was in Italy that one of France's master confectioners learnt the art of the frozen dessert. Early in his career, probably in 1659, Nicolas Audiger travelled to Italy to perfect his understanding of the craft of the sorbette maker. On his return to France, he spent untold hours trying to secure a nationwide monopoly on the production of these Italian-style treats but was stymied by his inability to navigate the complex web of patronage and nepotism that governed such things. While remaining constantly irritated by his failure to make a fortune from his confections, Audiger found his skills in high demand among the gluttonous bluebloods of Louis XIV's court. His reputation reached glorious heights in January 1687 when he was invited to contribute to a celebratory banquet to mark the Sun King's recovery from an operation on an anal fistula (the thought of which apparently did nothing to dampen the appetite of the extravagantly be-wigged attendees). To great excitement, the confectioner unveiled a 'portable collation of all manner of fruit, and waters, both liquid and frozen'.

In his book, *La Maison Réglée*, published the same year as Latini's, Audiger provided recipes for regular unfrozen 'sorbec de levant' (Levantine sherbets) in an array of flavours, and suggested that to freeze any of these, the quantity of sugar should be doubled and the fruits, flowers and seeds increased by half to make the flavours stand up to the cold. He also provided lengthy instructions for freezing, emphasising the importance of stirring to create a texture more like snow than ice and to prevent the sugar from settling. Among his recipes was one for an ice cream ('cresme glacée', as he called it) made from a mix of milk, cream, sugar and orange flower water – a citrusy distillate used extensively in North African cuisine, which for hundreds of years would remain as ubiquitous an ice cream flavouring as vanilla is now, providing a lasting echo of the dessert's exotic roots.

A contemporary of Audiger's, Francois Massialot, chef

to various dukes and cardinals and pioneer of both the meringue and the crème brûlée, was far less of a specialist in frozen desserts, but his influence would prove much greater. Massialot's book of dessert recipes, *Nouvelle Instruction pour les Confitures, les Liqueurs et les Fruits* (1692), featured just a handful of sweet ices, described in a rather cursory manner and with some pretty shaky instructions for freezing, but the book's reach – its recipes were reproduced in multiple languages, including a highly successful English translation, entitled *The Court and Country Cook* – far outstripped those of his more accomplished ice-making peers. One of Massialot's recipes was for a version of ice cream called 'fromage à l'Anglois' (English cheese). This was particularly notable for the presence of three egg yolks alongside the cream, milk and sugar: the first recorded appearance of an ingredient that would gradually become a near-universal component in both French and British ice cream, marking a significant break from the dessert's Italian roots. In their use of eggs, both countries were tapping into their long traditions of making sweet egg custards, in the same way that Italy's love of fruit sherbets shaped the development of the sorbetto. By contrast, Italian gelato – a word that only took root in the nineteenth century to differentiate milk ices from water ices – contains little if any egg.

While Italy remained the spiritual home of flavoured ices, it was in France that the laborious process of stirring and freezing ice cream was refined – or at least it was in France that this refinement was first recorded. According to Monsieur Emy, an otherwise unknown obsessive whose book about ice cream was published in Paris in 1768, the ices that had hitherto graced the tables of the rich were actually pretty terrible: light on flavour and as hard as concrete (an accusation borne out by a close reading of Massialot's instructions). To counter these flaws, he offered some incredibly detailed technical advice – his master recipe ran to three and a half pages – and followed this with dozens of flavour variations, including vanilla (which had only arrived from the New World in the sixteenth century and was far from ubiquitous), strawberry, chocolate, coffee, cinnamon, cloves, Maltese oranges, pineapple (which he called 'the king of fruits'), a spice mix called 'houacaca' and, most strikingly, truffle – a quarter of a pound of Perigord's finest.

The attention to detail demonstrated by Monsieur Emy had been sadly lacking from Britain's oldest recipe for ice cream, which was scribbled down decades before any of the afore-mentioned ice pioneers put pen to paper. Dated 1651–78, a manuscript of the jottings of Lady Ann Fanshawe, wife of the English ambassador to Spain, contained a recipe that, while historically notable, was entirely hopeless – it started well, with 'three pints of the best cream' boiled with mace, orange flower water or ambergris, then sweetened with sugar, but things went awry when Lady Ann's method for freezing the cream completely failed to mention salt. Follow her recipe to the letter, and you'll end up with a slightly chilled milkshake.

Presumably, whoever was responsible for the catering at a spectacular banquet in honour of the Order of the Garter, hosted at Windsor Castle in May 1671, understood a little better the mechanics of freezing. On the evening before the main feast and at the feast itself, the King's table was supplied with 'one plate of ice cream'. Nobody but Charles II himself was served with this delicacy – its first recorded appearance on an English menu. This exclusivity was telling: until the nineteenth century, ice cream remained a luxury. Ice – which had to be either harvested in the winter or shipped from colder climes, then carefully stored in heavily insulated ice pits or ice houses – was cripplingly expensive, while salt and clarified sugar were still far from cheap. All around Europe, water ices and ice creams became culinary status symbols at the tables of the mighty. As one Victorian food writer put it: 'Not so many years ago an ice pudding was looked upon as a triumph of culinary art, that even the average good professed cook would as soon have thought of trying to make, as of trying to fly.'

Given the rarefied status of ices, it befitted the chefs of grand households to present their creations in elaborate displays. Pewter moulds were fabricated to create pyramids, obelisks, fruits, flowers, artillery shells ('bombes') or – one popular Heston-like trick – cuts of meat. In 1781, John Moore, a British doctor based in Italy, who tagged along on a royal visit to one of the city's convents, described how the King and Queen of Naples were shown to a table laden with 'a most plentiful cold repast, consisting of several joints of meat, hams, fowl, fish, and various other dishes,' a surprising choice of spread given that dinner had already been taken. Moore wrote: 'The Queen chose a slice of cold turkey, which, on being cut up, turned out a large piece of lemon ice, of the shape and appearance of a roasted turkey. All the other dishes were ices of various kinds, disguised under the forms of joints of meat, fish, and fowl.' Queen

Victoria's Italian chef Charles Elmé Francatelli was also a fan of these incongruous presentations. His book *The Royal English and Foreign Confectionery Book* (1862) included detailed instructions for making an imitation ham and, even more elaborately, a boar's head 'made of Savoy biscuit and filled with ice cream' – a recipe that included the priceless note that 'if you can procure a mould of the natural shape of a wild boar's head . . . it would considerably facilitate your object'.

In Europe's most prosperous cities, including Paris, Vienna and London, ices could be procured in the grand cafes frequented by the wealthy. In 1759, an Italian confectioner, Domenico Negri, opened the Sign of the Pineapple on Berkeley Square in London's Mayfair, where the city's elite, including members of the royal family, gathered to consume 'all sorts of ice, fruits and creams in the best Italian manner'. Several of Negri's colleagues and apprentices, including James Gunter and Frederick Nutt, would go on to be important figures in the development of English ice cream and, thanks to the high-end nature of the trade, wealthy men. Nutt's book, *The Complete Confectioner*, published anonymously in 1789, was one of the best of the era and featured thirty recipes for ice creams, including many of the flavours that are still most closely associated with the British ice cream counter – strawberry, raspberry, chocolate, coffee, caramel ('burnt ice cream' as Nutt called it) – and one that definitely isn't: parmesan cheese.

The development that would finally bring this posh pudding to a wider audience was the increase in the availability and affordability of ice. In the first decades of the nineteenth century, aided by advances in the speed and scale of ocean-going ships, an international trade emerged from what had previously been, by necessity, a fairly localised industry. This was centred at first upon the seas around Greenland. Then, in the 1840s, the Wenham Lake Ice Company, based in Massachusetts, began the large-scale shipment of American ice to London and quickly began to dominate the market – a big block of crystal-clear ice, frequently replaced but to the untrained eye seemingly indestructible, was on display in the window of its premises on the Strand and became quite the attraction. The ease and relative cheapness with which ice could be purchased from Wenham Lake's multiple depots, combined with parallel developments in the sophistication of machinery for churning ice cream, made the mass production of ices suddenly viable.

Viable, but not instantly successful. According to Henry Mayhew, who surveyed the lives of the London poor in 1851, initial attempts at introducing ice cream as a street food were met with suspicion. One street dealer scoffed at the very notion that such a luxurious treat could find a place in the repertoire of his peers: 'Ices in the streets! Aye, and there'll be jellies next, and then mock turtle . . . penny glasses of champagne, I shouldn't wonder.' Another dealer who had attempted to sell ices was fairly negative about the whole experience. 'I don't think they'll ever take greatly in the streets,' he predicted. 'They get among the teeth and make you feel as if you tooth-ached all over.'

It didn't take long for such gloomy predictions to crumble. The second half of the nineteenth century saw a significant increase in migration from Italy to the towns and cities of the UK. Poor, unskilled migrants arriving from southern

Italy, a region steeped in ice cream lore, were far more convinced than Mayhew's cynical cockneys of the possibility of hawking frozen desserts, and the country's streets soon echoed with the cries of hawkers selling 'hokey pokey' – the name given, for reasons that have never been entirely convincingly explained, to the cheap, dense ice cream sold from carts by Italian vendors. Hokey pokey was, wrote Andrew Tuer in 1885, 'dreadfully sweet, dreadfully cold, and hard as a brick'. It was rumoured, he continued, that one of its base ingredients might be creamed swede (probably slanderous). Softer ice cream was sold on the streets as 'penny licks' – a small glass from which the customer licked their purchase before returning it to the seller to be rinsed in the most cursory of manners: a system implicated in a number of disease outbreaks. Thankfully, the rise in the early twentieth century of the edible wafer cone saved many an ice cream lover from this epidemiological menace.

Italy gave birth to the ice cream, France refined it and Britain turned it into street food, but it was the USA that wrote its most recent chapter. As with so many foodstuffs, the American drive to embrace new technologies, create systems of mass production and then exploit the magic of marketing to shape consumer tastes transformed our perceptions of ice cream. In 1922, T Wall's & Sons, a London-based sausage maker, used imported American machinery to create Britain's first industrial-scale ice cream business. Other ideas that crossed the Atlantic included the lolly on a stick, first patented in America in 1924, and the 'soft-serve' ice cream – developed in the United States in the 1930s, popularised here in the 1960s and, contrary to the popular myth, not invented by Margaret Thatcher – which cut back on all those gorgeous dairy fats and replaced them with cheap vegetable oil and even cheaper air. The UK continues to dance to that American tune, and most of the ice cream eaten here today is more industrial wizardry than natural magic.

As with so many foods, though, there are still ice cream makers among us who stick to the old ways, producing their wares in a manner that – electric power aside – would be recognisable to Frederick Nutt and his Georgian peers: beautiful natural ingredients, sweetened, churned and frozen. Many things have changed since Giambattista della Porta first recommended mixing saltpetre with ice, but – in the right hands – the potential for conjuring excitement from the chiller isn't one of them.

BIBLIOGRAPHY

Acton, Eliza. *Modern Cookery*. Longman, Brown, Green and Longman, 1845

al-Hasan, Muhammad; al-Karim, Muhammad. *A Baghdad Cookery Book* (trans Charles Perry). Prospect Books, 2005

Apicius. *Cookery and Dining in Imperial Rome* (trans Joseph Dommers Vehling). Dover Publications, 1978

Aristotle, *Historia Animalium* (trans D'Arcy Wentworth Thompson). Clarendon Press, 1910

Athenaeus. *The Deipnosophists* (trans CD Yonge). Henry Bohn, 1854

Badham, David. *Ancient and Modern Fish Tattle*. JW Parker, 1854

Bartolini, Giorgio; Petruccelli, Raffaella. *Classification, Origin, Diffusion and History of the Olive*. Food and Agriculture Organization of the United Nations, 2002

Bede. *Bede's Ecclesiastical History of England*. George Bell and Sons, 1907

Beeton, Isabella. *The Book of Household Management*. SO Beeton, 1861

Bertram, James G. *The Harvest of the Sea*. John Murray, 1869

Brovedani, Daniela; Tyfield, Susan (ed). *Pasta*. Barilla, 2000

Brown, Pete. *The Apple Orchard*. Penguin Books, 2017

Bunyard, Edward A. *The Anatomy of Dessert*. Modern Library, 2006

Columella. *Of Husbandry: In Twelve Books.* 1745

Columella. *On Agriculture* (trans ES Foster & Edward Heffner). William Heinemann, 1954

Dalby, Andrew. *Dangerous Tastes.* The British Museum Press, 2000

Dalby, Andrew. *Food in the Ancient World from A to Z.* Routledge, 2003

Darrow, George M. *The Strawberry.* The New England Institute for Medical Research, 1966

David, Elizabeth. *Harvest of the Cold Months.* Faber and Faber, 2012

David, Elizabeth. *Italian Food.* Penguin Books, 2011

Davidson, Allan. *The Oxford Companion to Food.* Oxford University Press, 1999

Davis, Nathaniel Newnham. *The Gourmet's Guide to Europe.* Brentano's, 1908

Day, Ivan. *Ice Cream.* Shire Publications, 2011

Day, Samuel Phillips. *Tea.* Simpkin, Marshall & Co, 1878

De Sahagún, Bernadino. *General History of the Things of New Spain* (trans Arthur JO Anderson & Charles E Dibble). University of Utah, 1970

De Vita, Oretta Zanini. *Encylopedia of Pasta* (trans Maureen B Fant). University of California Press, 2009

Defoe, Daniel. *Tour through the Eastern Counties of England, 1722.* Cassell & Company, 1891

Della Porta, Giambattista. *Natural Magick.* Young & Speed, 1658

Digby, Kenelm. *The Closet of Sir Kenelm Digby Knight Opened* Dodo Press, 2009

Dodd, James Solas. *An Essay Towards a Natural History of the Herring.* T Vincent, 1752

Dods, Margaret. *The Cook and Housewife's Manual.* 1826 & 1837

Dolby, Richard. *The Cook's Dictionary.* Colburn & Bentley, 1830

Eales, Mary. *Mrs Mary Eales's Receipts*. J Brindley, 1733

Ellis, Markman; Coulton, Richard; Mauger, Matthew. *Empire of Tea*. Reaktion Books, 2015

Ellis, Marksman (ed). *Eighteenth-Century Coffee-House Culture*. Routledge, 2016

Evelyn, John. *Acetaria*. Women's Auxiliary, 1937

Fort, Tom. *The Book of Eels*. HarperCollins, 2003

Frankopan, Peter. *The Silk Roads*. Bloomsbury, 2015

Frézier, Amédée François. *The Voyage to the South Sea*. Christian Bowyer, 1735

Galen. *On the Properties of Foodstuff* (trans Owen Powell). Cambridge University Press, 2003

Gentilcore, David. *Pomodoro!*. Columbia University Press, 2010

Gerard, John. *The Herball*. 1597

Glasse, Hannah. *The Art of Cookery*. 1747

Hakluyt, Richard. *The Principal Navigations, Voyages, Traffiques and Discoveries of the English Nation*. E&G Goldsmid, 1889

Hattox, Ralph S. *Coffee & Coffeehouses*. University of Washington Press, 1996

Herodotus. *The Histories* (trans AD Godley). Loeb Classical Library, 1920–5

Homer. *The Odyssey* (trans Samuel Butler). AC Fifield, 1900

Hurley, John. *The Tree, the Olive, the Oil in the Old and New World*. 1919

Ibn Battuta. *Travels in Asia and Africa* (trans HAR Gibb). George Routledge & Sons, 1929

Janick, Jules; Moore, James N (ed). *Fruit Breeding*. John Wiley & Sons, 1996

Jay, Martha. *Onions and Garlic*. Reaktion Books, 2016

Jenkins, Virginia Scott. *Bananas*. Smithsonian Institution Press, 2000

Kiple, Kenneth F; Ornelas, Kriemhild Coneè. *The Cambridge World History of Food*. Cambridge University Press, 2000

Koehler, Jeff. *Darjeeling*. Bloomsbury, 2015

Koeppel, Dan. *Banana*. Plume, 2008

Kurlansky, Mark. *Salt*. Vintage, 2003

Longe, Francis D. *Lowestoft in Olden Times*. McGregor & Fraser, 1899

Lydgate, John. *Mummings and Entertainments* (ed Claire Sponsler). Kalamazoo, 2010

Maestro Martino of Como. *The Art of Cooking* (trans Jeremy Parzen). University of California Press, 2005

Markham, Gervase. *The English Huswife*. R Jackson, 1623

Mayhew, Henry. *London Labour and the London Poor*. Griffin, Bohn and Company, 1851–61

McCabe, Ina Baghdiantz. *A History of Global Consumption 1500–1800*. Routledge, 2015

Milne, AH. *Sir Alfred Lewis Jones*. Henry Young & Sons, 1914

Mitchell, John M. *The Herring*. Edmonston & Douglas, 1864

Morgan, Jean; Richards, Alison. *The New Book of Apples*. Ebury Press, 2002

Mueller, Tom. *Extra Virginity*. Atlantic Books, 2012

Myers, Gordon. *Banana Wars*. Zed Books, 2004

Nott, John. *The Cooks and Confectioners Dictionary*. C Rivington, 1723

Parkinson, John. *Paradisi in Sole Paradisus Terrestris*. 1629

Pegge, Samuel (ed). *The Forme of Cury*. Forgotten Books, 2008

Pendergast, Mark. *Uncommon Grounds*. Basic Books, 2010

Pliny the Elder. *The Natural History* (trans John Bostock and HT Riley). HG Bohn, 1855–7

Plutarch. *Moralia* (trans Frank Cole Babbitt). William Heinemann, 1957

Randolph, Mary. *The Virginia Housewife*. John Plaskitt, 1836

Rangeley-Wilson, Charles. *Silver Shoals*. Chatto & Windus, 2018

Riley, Gillian. *The Oxford Companion to Italian Food*. Oxford University Press, 2009

Rodinson, Maxime; Perry, Charles; Arberry, Arthur J. *Medieval Arab Cookery*. Prospect Books, 2006.

Russell, John. *The Boke of Nurture*. John Childs & Don, 1867

Salmon, William. *Pharmacopoeia Bateana*. Smith & Walford, 1694

Scappi, Bartolomeo. *The Opera of Bartolomeo Scappi* (trans Terence Scully). University of Toronto Press, 2008

Schweid, Richard. *Consider the Eel*. The University of North Carolina Press, 2010

Serventi, Silvano; Sabban, Françoise. *Pasta* (trans Antony Shuggar). Columbia University Press, 2002

Shephard, Sue. *Pickled, Potted, and Canned* Headline Books, 2000

Smith, Andrew F. *The Tomato in America*. University of Illinois Press, 2001

Smith, Andrew F. *The Turkey: An American Story*. University of Illinois Press, 2012

Smith, Simon. *A Narrative of the Royal Fishings of Great Britain and Ireland*. W Godbid, 1661

Smylie, Mike. *Herring*. The History Press, 2004

Solieri, Lisa; Giudici, Paolo (ed). *Vinegars of the World*. Springer, 2009

Strabo. *The Geography* (trans HL Jones). Harvard University Press, 1917–32

Swartz, Wendy; Campany, Robert Ford; Lu, Yang; Choo, Jessey JC. *Early Medieval China*. Columbia University Press, 2014

Theophrastus. *Enquiry into Plants* (trans Arthur Holt). Harvard University Press, 1916

Thomas, Hugh. *The Slave Trade*. Picador, 1997

Thurber, Francis B. *Coffee*. American Grocer Publishing Association, 1881

Turner, Jack. *Spice*. HarperCollins, 2004

Ukers, William H. *All About Coffee*. The Tea and Coffee Trade Journal Company, 1922

Ukers, William H. *All About Tea*. The Tea and Coffee Trade Journal Company, 1935

Van Driem, George. *The Tale of Tea*. Brill, 2019

Walton, Izaak. *The Compleat Angler*. Richard Marriot, 1653

Weir, Caroline; Weir, Robin. *Ice Creams, Sorbets & Gelati*. Grub Street, 2010

Wissett, Robert. *A View of the Rise, Progress, and Present State of the Tea Trade in Europe*. 1801

ABOUT
BOROUGH MARKET

Around a thousand years ago – almost six hundred years before John Gerard started growing tomatoes in the London suburb of Holborn and a full nine centuries before boatloads of bananas started to be unloaded from the Thames – a food market took shape at the southern end of London Bridge, then the sole crossing into the city. In one form or another, Borough Market has been here ever since.

In 1756, the Market moved to its current location just off the high street. In 1998, after the rise of the super-markets had put paid to its once mighty fruit and veg wholesale operation, Borough was reborn as a retail market offering a clear alternative to the increasingly industrialised mainstream. Run by a charitable trust, its current mission is to provide access to food of exceptional quality, made and sold in a way that places value on people and the planet. Many of its traders grow, rear or make the food they sell; others use their knowledge of specific regions or foodstuffs to source exceptional products directly from small-scale producers in Britain, Europe and further afield. With its colourful, dynamic community of traders, trustees, staff, customers, chefs, writers and supporters, the Market is helping to shape the growing public interest in the quality, provenance, ethics and sustainability of the food we eat.

www.boroughmarket.org.uk

ACKNOWLEDGEMENTS

Thanks to the editorial and design team at Hodder & Stoughton – Liz Gough, Liv Nightingall, Kay Halsey, Will Speed – for making all this happen, to Emily Langford for the pitch-perfect illustrations, and to Zoe Ross at United Agents for bringing us all together.

Thanks to the management, staff and trustees at Borough Market for their impressive commitment to telling stories, sharing knowledge and engaging with the public as well as selling produce, and for the wonderful opportunities they have given me over the years.

Thanks to Kate Howell, Claire Ford and the LSC team for the creativity and teamwork that have made producing this book – as well as *Market Life* and the many other projects we've worked on together – such a consistent pleasure.

Thanks to the fantastic community of traders without whose deep commitment and unparalleled expertise Borough Market would just be a big empty shed on the side of the Thames. Everything we do starts with them, and much of what we do ends with me eating some of their cheese, charcuterie or cake.

Thanks to my good friend Richard and several members

of my immediate family for giving up their time to read about food rather than just stuffing their faces with it, and for the very useful feedback they gave. And thanks to Sarah for, well, everything really, not least her support, encouragement and impressive ability to refrain from sighing when, over dinner, I roll out the same story about eels or strawberries she's heard a dozen times before.